VAX to VAX

VAX to VAX

A Practical Guide to Connecting VAXs and their Peripherals

Corey Sandler
Tom Badgett

John Wiley & Sons, Inc.

NEW YORK / CHICHESTER / BRISBANE / TORONTO / SINGAPORE

Library of Congress Cataloging in Publication Data:

Sandler, Corey. 1950–
     VAX to VAX: a practical guide to connecting VAXs and
     their peripherals / Corey Sandler.
  Tom Badgett.
       p.   cm.
     Includes bibliographical references.
     1. Local area networks (Computer networks) 2. VAX computers
  3. Computer interfaces. 4. Computer network protocols.
  I. Badgett, Tom. II. Title.
  TK5105.7.S26 1990
  621.39'8--dc20   90-12208
  ISBN 0-471-51506-X   CIP

Printed in the United States of America

10 9 8 7 6 5 4 3 2 1

To Mellryn,
where synergy works for us.

CONTENTS

PREFACE

In a way, the title of *VAX to VAX Communications* for this book is redundant. VAX *is* communications.

The engine that brought Digital Equipment Corporation to prominence is the Virtual Address Extended (VAX) architecture, a concept that allows the system manager to think of a room full of computers, or a company full of computers, or even a number of distant individual machines as one entity.

The concepts of distributed processing, networking, shared access, and electronic mail are well established today. Computer hardware, software, and networking vendors routinely plan for a global computing environment.

But a look at the history of Digital VAXs shows that this architecture obviously led the way; everything else has been modeled on it. Other minicomputers, and even the PC revolution—despite Digital's own reluctance to embrace the PC itself—have come around to Digital's way of thinking.

BACKGROUND

The growth of large, central computer systems in the 1970s was one of the reasons for the rapid acceptance of "personal" computing platforms as the technology became available.

As more and more people got accustomed to the concept of attaching directly to company-level or departmental-level computer power, they began to demand more control over available functions, software style and capability, and even hardware features.

Understandably, MIS departments became backlogged. They simply couldn't respond to the volume of end user requests and needs fast enough, and all too often the perception by users was that the people controlling their computer access didn't want to cooperate with them.

Indeed, as computers moved into departments and onto desktops—frequently without the knowledge or sanction of MIS personnel—the two groups frequently faced off across a scrimmage line of different goals and expectations. MIS felt the necessity of maintaining control over the corporate computing environment. End users and sometimes whole departments felt they couldn't wait any longer to achieve the computing goals they knew were possible.

In many companies this conflict was not resolved. Where possible, desktop users established their own individual and networked computing entities, breaking away from the central computing environment for everything but established processes that were not easily replaced.

As traditional computing personnel learned more about the desktop phenomenon, they accepted it somewhat, and the intensity of the face-off between users and MIS began to soften. Through the middle and late 1980s a lot of give-and-take on the part of desktop aficionados took place as well. And, of course, standards and technology across all facets of the computer industry grew to broaden the possibilities available to all computer classes.

TODAY'S COMPUTING ENVIRONMENT

Today there is a push to get all computers, large and small, connected in a cohesive, comprehensive, cooperative enterprise that draws on the strengths of each component. Among the benefits of tying various computing entities together are electronic mail, shared storage, automatic backup, common user interfaces, and applications.

In addition, today's Digital Equipment Corporation computers, coupled with the latest applications software, support distributed processing. This concept lets computation take place close to where it is needed, or where the data are located. By distributing processing among various CPUs, the joined computers form a computing environment that is more powerful than any of its components. And the cost of building CPU power this way frequently is less than that of installing a single large processor.

Again, this was part of the VAX concept from the beginning, a concept that is maturing and fitting nicely within the national and international standards now settling into place.

The key to the success of this communications concept is the standardization in hardware and software that vendors such as Digital and others have evolved over the years. The VAX hardware platform, when coupled with VMS and Ultrix operating systems, forms a powerful and "universal" computing environment.

THE DIGITAL PHILOSOPHY

Because of Digital's general computing philosophy, it is among the first companies to provide such a comprehensive linked environment. Today, with third party vendors supporting Digital hardware and software, and with the work by OSI (Open Systems Interconnect) and other bodies, what was only an elusive dream is rapidly becoming reality.

For example, the industry acceptance of the X Window System user and applications interface eventually will provide a standard link between the desktop and the CPU, whether the actual processor is located next door or on another continent. Digital's implementation, DECWindows, comes with applications toolkits and desktop applications that make a $1 million VAX as easy and friendly to use as a $2,000 PC.

In addition to the basic communications orientation of the VAX computer, the foundation of Digital's computing platform is DECnet, an Ethernet-based communications protocol. Among the interesting facts about DECnet is that it grew out of the company's own need to link its computers for development and application sharing. As the hardware and software evolved and it was offered to the general computing public, DECnet became an important part of what makes a VAX a VAX. DECnet is obviously an important part of what the book is about because it is an integral part of the physical and logical link that ties one VAX to another.

Without a strong computing network structure you lose on-demand information access. And, after all, it is information, perhaps as much as any other single factor, that drives a company's success. Digital Equipment Corporation, in *A Common Sense Guide to Network Management*, describes the role of strong corporate computer networking this way:

> Just as it is important to ensure the liquidity of monetary assets, so also it is crucial to the success of the company to ensure the liquidity of information; that is, to enable information to flow easily and quickly through the enterprise.
>
> Networks do this. Senior managers can make significant decisions that are timely and well-informed. Individuals and departments within the enterprise can share resources across networks. Productivity improves and resources are more efficiently utilized. Networks can greatly speed product development and enable quick response to customer needs. In general, networks enable a corporation to seize market advantage.

For Digital, networking is an integral part of corporate as well as marketing philosophy. The company has one of the largest networks in the world. In fact, the network is part of corporate culture, linking employees and departments in a global enterprise. Almost any employee almost anywhere in the world can reach almost anyone else in the company. This capability builds community, and enables teams comprising employees separated by half a world to work together on projects.

In addition, this corporate network enhances the computer power available for any given task. Work groups and departments have the processors they need close at hand, but they share CPUs and data from around the enterprise as well.

Distributed processing is the basis of Digital's computing philosophy. The network and its support components are all part of a computing whole that is used within the company and promoted to customers as part of the Digital VAX package.

This is the environment we are talking about in this book, the leading edge of Digital computer-to-computer communications. Today, network backbones that tie together the large components of a commercial enterprise are essential to competitive strength.

If you already are using a corporate network, this book will help you understand how it functions and how to get more out of what you have. If you are just starting to link people and processes, the information in this book will help you plan the work and work the plan.

Either way, we hope you come away with a sense of the importance of VAX-to-VAX communication and all of the side issues it entails, and maybe even a little wonder at the concept of a global enterprise and the power and functionality that such a system places in the hands of individuals.

Holliston, Massachusetts   Corey Sandler

Corryton, Tennessee   Tom Badgett

April 1990

ACKNOWLEDGMENTS

The authors note with thanks the contributions of some of the people and companies who helped with this book.

Thanks to Tracy Smith at Waterside Productions for her capable agentry; to John Wiley & Sons for publishing the book; and to the numerous folk at Digital for supplying information and answering questions.

Thanks to our families for their understanding and cooperation. Any vocation you pursue at home—but perhaps writing more than some—is a group effort.

We also wish to acknowledge the valuable assistance provided by a number of major hardware and software companies. We commend their products to your attention.

This book was researched and prepared using equipment and software that included the following:

Austin 286/16. An 80286-based personal computer with built-in VGA graphics support, 4 Mbytes of RAM, and a 40 Mbyte hard disk. Austin Computer Systems, 10300 Metric Blvd., Austin, TX 78758 (800) 752-1577.

CompuAdd 386/20. A 20-MHz 80386 PC with 0 wait state, cache memory. CompuAdd Corporation, 12303 Technology Blvd., Austin, TX 78727 (800) 627-1967.

CompuAdd 316S computer. A 16 MHz, 80386SX computer with 1 Mbyte of RAM and a 150 Mbtye IDE hard disk; VGA monitor. CompuAdd Corporation.

Fujitsu RX7100PS. PostScript LED printer. Fujitsu America, Inc., 3055 Orchard Drive, San Jose, CA 95134 (408) 432-1300.

Lanlink Version 5.0, serial network for printer and file sharing. The Software Link, Inc., 3577 Parkway Lane, Atlanta, GA 30092 (404) 448-5465.

NEC Silentwriter LC-890 PostScript LED printer. NEC Information Systems, Inc., 1414 Massachusetts Avenue, Boxboro, MA 01719 (508) 264-8000.

Swan 386/20 Computer. A 20 MHz, 80386 computer with 0 wait state memory, shadow bios, and a 150 Mbyte hard drive. Tussey Computer Products, 3075 Research Drive, State College, PA 16801 (800) 468-9044.

Word Version 5.0 word processing software. Microsoft Corporation, 16011 NE 36th Way, Box 97017, Redmond, WA 98073-9717.

C. S.
T. B.

CHAPTER 1

Introduction

THE CONCEPT
WHAT THIS BOOK IS ABOUT
WHO SHOULD READ THIS BOOK
CONVENTIONS USED IN THIS BOOK
WHAT IS IN THIS BOOK

Few VAXs ever stand alone. The basis of Digital Equipment Corporation's computer philosophy is that the VAX means connectivity. Digital pushes the network almost as much as the VAX itself. In addition, third-party hardware and software vendors are developing products that take advantage of the VAX's ability to communicate with other VAXs and the ability of PCs, workstations, and other devices to communicate with the resultant multi-VAX configuration.

THE CONCEPT

Look around you. If you are sitting in a typical office, you are within easy reach of various electronic communications devices. In addition to the telephone—a ubiquitous and vital business and personal link for everyone today—there is probably a FAX machine nearby. You are likely to see at least one PC or other desktop computer that includes a dial-up modem link to the host computers in your own company and to the machines at hundreds of other companies across the country and around the world.

If you are a VAX user, the terminal at your desk is communicating to a host computer, either directly to a serial or network port on the VAX or to a terminal server that in turn communicates to the VAX.

Moreover, the VAX you spend most of your time accessing is probably attached over DECnet to one or more additional VAXs, mainframes, computer services, diagnostic processors, or other intelligent devices.

Ours is a communicating society. We use sophisticated business and personal tools in every facet of our lives. In a business environment so interconnected and interdependent, it seems fitting that individuals have resources to inform them about the functions of the system on which they depend for livelihood.

Today, people who have no experience in the field are being called on to justify networking resources to link their departmental or individual CPU to the rest of the corporation through a mainframe or multiple department link. They are serving on committees to design departmental or corporate networks; they are attempting to answer questions about linking individual desktop computers to a corporate network; they are using interconnected systems during the conduct of their everyday work.

Yet in most businesses the documentation for the computer resources they are using is safely sequestered in the manager's office or computer room. The one available copy of each manual may be in use by someone else when you need it, or it may simply be locked up while the manager is out to lunch.

As the manager of a growing department, and as a user of networked Digital hardware, you need a concise, inexpensive guide to the general concepts of Digital networking.

That need was the origin of this book. Here we have attempted to outline the major concepts behind computer-to-computer communication in the Digital world.

WHAT THIS BOOK IS ABOUT

This book is about computer communication. It provides a broad overview of VAX-to-VAX communications and demonstrates how the VAX architecture can fit with others, including PCs and Macintosh machines.

Given the scope of this project, we can't possibly answer every question on the topic, nor will you be able to configure a communications system straight from this book. For that level of detail you will need help from Digital publications, your local Digital sales representative, consultants, and people inside your firm. But the material in this book will get you started, providing a foundation for discussion as you move from stand-alone hardware to a fully networked environment.

WHO SHOULD READ THIS BOOK

This book is for anyone interested in linking multiple VAX computers or in tying VAXs to PCs and other desktop devices. If you are a seasoned network expert and fully familiar with the VAX communications environment, you will be on familiar ground.

You can use this book as a teaching tool for other members of your department and as a resource for planning committees as you design or expand networking in your company.

If you are a terminal user and you'd like to know a little about how the multiple computers in your organization function together, we can help. The discussions of DECnet and communications protocols will tell you a little about how the various CPUs in your shop work. Refer to the section on terminal servers and serial communication for some background on how serial devices attach to the VAX.

CONVENTIONS USED IN THIS BOOK

Describing computer concepts and interaction with a computer can be difficult unless it is agreed in advance how certain things will be handled. This section outlines some of the general conventions used in this book. Others should be obvious as you read through the material.

Digital = Digital Equipment Corporation. Although in years past it has been common to refer to this company as DEC, and while some Digital products still carry this moniker (DECwindows, DECnet, DEConnect), the company is making a concerted public effort to replace DEC with Digital. Therefore, to remain consistent with company practice and policy, we will use Digital, not DEC, to refer to Digital Equipment Corporation.

Control Characters. Throughout this book, control characters will be indicated with the following convention:

Ctrl-A (for example) for the character yielded by holding down the Ctrl key and typing the letter *a*.

Shift-Ctrl-A for a character yielded by holding down the Ctrl key and Shift key and then typing the letter *a*.

The Alt key is used in the same way as the Ctrl key to provide an alternate character set or command code. Alt-key combinations will be indicated in the same way as control characters; for example:

Alt-A represents the character yielded by holding down the Alt key and typing the letter *a*.

Shifted Characters. Shifted characters will be indicated with the following convention:

Shift-A (for example) for the character yielded by holding down either of the Shift keys and typing the letter *a*.

PC and Workstation. These terms are merging in general use. Although there may be some subtle differences in some applications, and purists will argue that a workstation is more powerful than a PC, the increasing power of personal computer devices makes this argument less and less valid. In this book we tend to use the terms PC and workstation interchangeably, except where there are obvious differences in application or performance requirements.

PC-DOS/MS-DOS. PC-DOS is IBM's compatible implementation of Microsoft's MS-DOS operating system for microcomputers. In this book, we will use the term MS-DOS to represent both IBM and IBM-compatible systems.

X Window System. The official term for the MIT-developed computer windowing standard is X Window System. Various publications and users generally shorten this to X Windows or simply to X. Wherever possible we will use the full name—X Window System. When that becomes unnecessarily cumbersome we also will shorten it to X Windows, but not to X.

WHAT IS IN THIS BOOK

Chapter 2: The VAX Computing Environment. A description of the major communications considerations in the VAX environment. Includes a detailed discussion of CDA, compound document architecture.

Chapter 3: DECWindows. An introduction to the X Window System and Digital's implementation, DECwindows. Includes information on X Terminals, a new technology that is bringing the benefits of the X Window System to more VAX users.

Chapter 4: Networking in the VAX Environment. A discussion of Digital's philosophy of VAX-to-VAX communication as well as the technology involved in linking VAXs. Includes a description of the OSI influence on DECnet and details the OSI networking layers.

Chapter 5: How Do You Connect? A summary of the major physical connection methods in VAX-to-VAX communications. Includes a detailed description of Digital's DECnet and some of its supporting hardware and software.

Chapter 6: Serial Communications. A detailed discussion of serial communications facilities and procedures. Includes information on dial-up links, modems, and direct connections.

Chapter 7: Network Checklist. A discussion of 15 vital questions you should ask during network planning and configuration. Provides information on network cabling, including FDDI fiber optics technology.

Chapter 8: PC-VAX Communications. The technology of PC-to-VAX links, including a discussion of specific IBM compatible and Apple desktop hardware. Includes a focus section to help VAX users interpret the PC's position in the VAX environment.

Chapter 9: Other Communications Environments. An annotated list of Digital and third-party communications environments that supplement basic DECnet. Also includes a description of remote diagnostics for VAXs and networks.

Chapter 10: Communications Security. A discussion of potential security problems in a networked environment and suggestions on how to avoid them. Includes a discussion of the DES encryption standard.

Appendix A: Serial Communications Reference. A summary of serial communications standards, cable connections, and procedures. Includes drawings and diagrams to illustrate cable wiring and explains Centronics parallel cables.

Appendix B: Modem Reference.   A summary of modem operation and selection criteria. Includes description of common modem standards and AT command codes.

Glossary.   A communications glossary. Use it to help you understand terms in this book and as a reference when you work with network configurations and operations.

The VAX Computing Environment

Digital Equipment Corporation's VAX, introduced in 1977, is probably the world's most successful single line of minicomputers. Based on a solid hardware design and supported by systems-level and applications software, VAXs are finding comfortable niches in engineering, scientific, business, and education installations.

The other interesting aspect of VAX computers, and one that has contributed to the success of the line, is Digital's communications philosophy, which stresses interoperability and distributed computing.

In this chapter we provide a general overview to the VAX line and some of the operating system and communications software that support it.

VAX HARDWARE

WHAT IS A VAX?

VAX stands for virtual address extension. The design grew out of Digital's original PDP (programmable data processor) family of minicomputers. The most advanced member of that series, the PDP-11, was built around a 16-bit processor that limited programmers to 64K-byte memory segments.

The VAX, on the other hand, uses a 32-bit processor and supports up to 4 billion memory address spaces. But the VAX added another feature, virtual addressing, so the machine can address (access) memory throughout the possible range, even if the physical memory inside the computer isn't that large. This offers an essentially unlimited amount of memory for users. Figure 2.1 shows a VAX 6000-460, which supports multiprocessing.

The VAX's memory management circuitry loads and stores programs in segments as they are needed and translates virtual memory addresses to physical addresses. Because there may not be enough physical memory to run all the programs being used at any one time, the VAX processor switches among processes very fast.

Each program appears to have the processor's full attention at any given time, but in reality each process is halted periodically

FIGURE 2.1   VAX 6000-460. One of Digital's newest VAXs supports multiprocessing. [Reprinted with permission of Digital Equipment Corporation.]

while the computer works on others. As a user or programmer, you don't notice this pause in processing unless things get very busy when many people and programs are all vying for CPU service. During these times you may notice slower response times, but the functionality remains, even though many users are sharing the CPU power and a limited amount of physical memory.

VAX OPERATING SYSTEMS

Some observers believe one key to Digital's success is an early decision to standardize on a single operating system and to maintain hardware compatibility with that software across a developing line of VAX computers. Coupled with that is a consistent commitment to networking with DECnet for applications software and data sharing.

The primary VAX operating system is VMS™(virtual memory system). VMS supports timesharing, batch processing, and real-time operations.

Ultrix, Digital's version of UNIX, is also available. Ultrix is an implementation of AT&T's System V UNIX, extended with Berkeley 4.2 functions. The perception in the industry for some time—and, indeed, within some departments of Digital itself— has been that Ultrix had a much lower marketing priority than VMS. That mood has changed with the release during 1989 of RISC machines based on Ultrix. A renewed marketing push for Ultrix systems and support for them has surfaced in the company within the past several months.

UNIX, in its many versions, is frequently perceived as a universal language because of the promise, at least, of language compatibility and continuity across many product lines.

Like any standard, however, there are inconsistencies in the way it is implemented by various vendors. There has been a lot of discussion in Digital circles recently over Ultrix and its place in the Digital product line. The company sells fewer Ultrix systems than it does VMS systems, but even before releasing its new RISC line, Ultrix formed a significant portion of Digital's overall sales. Moreover, the importance of Ultrix to Digital and its customers will increase with the popularity of UNIX, which today is gaining user acceptance as an operating system that provides programmer and user continuity across heterogeneous hardware lines.

At the same time the proprietary VMS operating system will likely remain the most popular operating system for VAXs. One reason is the close fit between the hardware and the software. The VAX and VMS were made for each other; they make an efficient, high-performance combination. And, as the Digital product line expands, VMS is expanding with it, making the proprietary solution more attractive.

In addition, such developments as standards-based networking (OSI) and DECwindows, a user interface that operates across VMS, Ultrix, and MS-DOS operating systems, are narrowing the differences in operating systems at the application and development level. These advances may, in fact, strengthen the position of proprietary operating systems from all vendors.

COMMUNICATIONS OVERVIEW

A number of basic building blocks provide a foundation for communicating in a VAX environment. The backbone of VAX connections is DECnet, Digital's proprietary networking protocol that rides on Ethernet. VAXs can talk to one another through high-speed cluster attachments, serial connections, or gateways and routers that link individual LANs (local area networks) or incompatible systems.

DECNET

DECnet is a proprietary communications protocol that rides over Ethernet cables. DECnet LANs connect VAXs, workstations, and even some third-party products that are DECnet-compatible. Digital supports the IEEE 802.3 Ethernet standard for hardware LAN connections over thickwire or thinwire coax, twisted pair, and optical cable for baseband LANs. VAX users can also use broadband networking for installations where video, voice, and other data communications need to be mixed on the same medium. See a more complete discussion of DECnet in Chapter 3.

VAX CLUSTERS

One of the tightest connections you can have between two VAXs is the VAX Cluster. There are several configurations for this high-speed Digital communications method. A special cluster bus or an Ethernet connection can be used to allow clustered VAXs to share storage and printer resources.

Clustering allows the attachment of up to 42 VAX systems and intelligent storage controllers. One of the main features of a clustered system is the sharing of large disk systems through high-speed intelligent links. Moreover, a clustered system allows the sharing of CPU power, generating a system more powerful than any of its individual parts.

In fact, Digital offers preconfigured clusters, marketed as single systems that the company describes as "flexible and efficient alternatives to mainframes."

Initially some Digital and third-party software could not always take advantage of the power of a clustered system. Today, however, databases, database-based applications, and other applications are catching up. For applications that require the maximum processing power and the ability to add CPUs over time, a clustered system could be a good choice.

For more detailed information on the cluster bus and the operation of clustered systems, see Chapter 4.

SERIAL CONNECTIONS

DECnet and other communications protocols don't necessarily have to run over Ethernet. In some applications, synchronous or asynchronous serial communications can provide the connections required.

Of course the most common way for an individual user to access a VAX host is over a serial line with a VT-series terminal or a terminal emulator platform such as a PC or Macintosh computer. This is not strictly a VAX-to-VAX link, but because VAXs riding on DECnet are tightly integrated and, with the proper applications, distribute their processing power, when you attach to a VAX network you are conducting VAX-to-VAX communications even if you are sitting at a lone serial terminal.

Additionally, DECnet can run over serial lines—serial DECnet—if you can tolerate slower speeds. Many dial-up and dedicated serial line users attach into the DECnet environment this way.

See Chapter 6 for more information on serial links in the VAX environment.

NETWORK-TO-NETWORK COMMUNICATIONS

Just as users of individual systems, including PCs and departmental VAXs, benefit from computer-to-computer links, these groups sometimes need access to other work groups within the same location or at sites around the world.

In this case you use a variety of network-to-network devices to turn a series of local groups into a larger enterprise. Digital and third-party routers shunt information among LANs at different locations. Various configurations of routers and converters can attach resources at local, regional, or far-flung locations.

Depending on the frequency and volume of data exchange among individual networks and the location of the various enterprise members, you might use dial-up communications, dedicated lines, public networks, even microwave or satellite links.

DECWINDOWS

Today more than ever the quality of the user interface to minicomputer operating systems and applications is an important issue. Thanks to work by standards groups and the cooperation of a number of companies in the computer market, a multitasking graphical user interface is becoming the norm.

The X Window System is the basis of Digital's DECwindows user environment as well as the user interface schemes of most major vendors today. These user interfaces offer excellent access to local and distributed applications and help link the hardware and software of various vendors across the network.

Digital's implementation, DECwindows, comes with a number of desktop applications. For more information on DECwindows and the X Window System environment, see Chapter 3.

COMPOUND DOCUMENT ARCHITECTURE (CDA)

Closely tied to DECwindows development is Digital's Compound Document Architecture™ or CDA. This is another move toward standardization in an important field of computer applications that will change user perception of data and computer applications in general.

Digital defines a compound document as a unified collection of data that can be edited, formatted, or otherwise processed as a document. Compound documents can contain a number of integrated components, including proportionally-spaced text, synthetic graphics, and scanned images. That is, a compound document is a document that has the ability to contain not only text but also integrated components. Compound documents can also contain data elements from applications such as spreadsheets. (From the Digital Compound Document Architecture Manual.)

So a compound document is a facility by which all components of documents can be made to integrate neatly into a desired format and processed easily via communications channels or converted to another format for transmission. Such is the mission of CDA.

This goal has been a gleam in the eye of MIS for some time, but only recently have the distributed computer power and communications capability required come together. Hardware communications have been adequately taken care of, but universal transfer of data has become a greater problem as the use of widely diversified software has proliferated.

Users in the Apple Macintosh and PC world are enjoying this type of integrated facility with such programs as InterMedia (see Figure 2.2). Digital's CDA and communication posture is moving rapidly toward giving workstation users just this type of capability. CDA and enhanced communications are helping it happen.

Currently the common denominator for text-based data has been ASCII (the American Standard for Coded Information Interchange). ASCII has also been used as a format for graphic information consisting of vector drawings (lines and boxes). The increasing use of more complex graphical information has created a plethora of information standards, however, multiplying problems in the transfer of a variety of textual and graphical information. The evolution of compound documents has amplified the need for a universal standard on which to base all data, textual or graphical.

Digital officials have stated that the company sees CDA as "the ASCII of the future." The general goal, according to the company, is to make it as easy in the future to handle compound documents as it is to handle ASCII text today. Although ASCII is a standard for document interchange among different hardware and software platforms, it can be quite cumbersome.

FIGURE 2.2   InterMedia Software running under A/UX on Apple Macintosh computers is providing access to multiple data types. Digital's CDA and supporting software is taking VAX users down this same path. [Courtesy of Apple Computer, Inc.]

One reason is the wide number of applications and data types: text, graphics, and images, from a number of sources among many different desktops. CDA will provide a solution to the current problem of transporting compound documents, including graphical elements, across different platforms among many users in different locations.

In Digital's view CDA is a complete environment that goes beyond just creating a compound document. The CDA environment includes the ability to distribute information among users no matter what kind of desktop device they are using, easily print it, display it, and create an entire environment that is very easy to handle from the user perspective.

The exciting aspect of CDA, taken to its ultimate goal, is the ability to sit at a network node—terminal, workstation, or PC—

and access text and graphics files, scanned images, photographs, sound, even motion video. These "document" types can ultimately be integrated into database, spreadsheet, and word processing files. When you combine these capabilities with color displays and printing, multiple window, multitasking screens, and high-speed networking, you can see that the face of end-user computing is obviously changing rapidly.

HOW DOES IT WORK?

It would be difficult to detail exactly how CDA works since it is dependent on other translating components to be effective. However, simplification will serve to promote an overall perspective of its functionality. Digital defines Compound Document Architecture as an entity that "provides a set of tools and utilities that simplify the treatment of compound document information."

The company appears to be very careful to make its definitions friendly and "organic." It is serious about the integration of CDA into data processing, and it is careful not to be intimidating or overt in its position. Digital will provide converters and tool kits for CDA that will allow even MS-DOS developers to create applications that output documents in the CDA format, DDIF specifically, free of charge (see Figure 2.3). The CDA Manual and Toolkit, which includes some software for CDA integration, will also be distributed free of charge to users of VMS and Ultrix and to software developers in an effort to get this standard established.

CDA works through a set of converters designed to address major formats. There is a converter at the front end, or input side, to accept documents in a supported format. These documents are then processed in a converter kernel to an output file of any supported format. Of note here is the supported format. For CDA to work to users' advantage, a number of formats must be supported. The more formats supported, the greater the use of CDA as a universal translator.

A more direct explanation is that the converter reads the input file, translates it to a DDIF in-memory format, and then translates this in-memory format to a specified output format. Any

DIGITAL EQUIPMENT CORPORATION'S CDA™

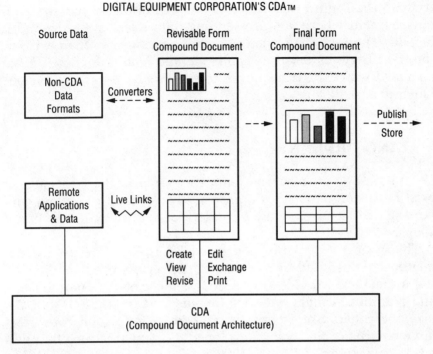

FIGURE 2.3 Digital's Compound Document Architecture provides data conversion through translators and supports live links to many popular applications. [Reprinted with permission of Digital Equipment Corporation.]

input file-encoding format that is supported by the CDA converter can be translated to a DDIF in-memory format, and this in-memory format can subsequently be converted to any supported output file-encoding format. DDIF is the standard being promoted by Digital as the document standard of choice, because DDIF documents can contain text, graphics, and images.

Digital is not the only vendor moving toward CDA capability. Some software companies, including Applix, Inc., in Westboro, MA, have been using their own CDA formats for some time. The Alis software supports live links among applications, including text, graphics, and database components. The company is bringing the system into compliance with Digital's CDA scheme.

Applix will not replace its existing standard with Digital's, the company says; rather, Applix software will provide compatibility with the Digital CDA functions. For example, if you are in an environment where you are sending data back and forth and it is using Digital's CDA, then information can be exchanged. The interface between existing Applix standards and the new Digital standard would be transparent to the user, even across various hardware platforms.

MAKING ORPHANS?

One of the major concerns for MIS people is the treatment of existing documents. With a growing list of major vendors supporting CDA, a move is indeed underfoot to utilize CDA in Digital shops.

This concern is firmly addressed by Digital. Existing documents are translated by a library of converters provided by Digital systems to provide conversion of most of the common text and graphics formats into CDA layouts. ASCII, DX, SGML, DCA, PIF, and others are among the standards for which converters are available or are being developed. For existing files that will need converting to CDA, the library of converters will enable the files to reach CDA form.

This conversion may be accomplished by first converting the files to another common format before converting them to CDA. Word processing files, for example, may need to be converted to DCA so that the DCA-CDA converter can be applied. The conversion is likely to take place on a VAX, but conversions are not inherently related to a particular platform.

Although converters will not exist for every word processing format, most formats should be accommodated in one of two ways. Many document formats will have converters to directly translate to another format. Others will require an intermediary step. For example, many word processing program formats have the capability of translating documents to the DCA format.

Doing so will enable the document to be converted through a CDA converter to another format; DDIF, for example. It is even conceivable that some less popular formats will require more than one conversion to be used in a CDA environment. Luckily, this would not have to be done often. The point being that most formats will be translatable. This should make life a bit easier for MIS directors and helps pave the way for CDA as a standard.

WHY CDA NOW?

It seems that some standard, some way of conveniently transferring all types of data, would have been available for some time,
but ASCII has basically been the sole means of commonly passing data for many years. One reason is that no notable tool has
come before it is needed. The need for a tool such as CDA has
never been greater than now.

In today's data processing scheme, there are more users,
more knowledgeable users, and more users performing more
tasks than ever before. Much of this is due to advancements in
software. Not too many years ago, only "power" users could com-
prehend much of the available software, and then assistance was
usually required to "bend" a program to fit an application.

The abundance of good software has lessened the need to form-
fit existing products through modification (modification is also
legally impossible these days anyhow), and much of the compro-
mise needed by MIS directors to fit their operations to a program
is also eliminated. In addition to database and word processing
activities, we now find more users involved with CAD/CAM/CAE,
and CASE (respectively: computer-aided design/computer-aided
manufacturing/computer-aided engineering, and computer-aided software engineering), which can require most elements of
data processing plus publishing.

This last category is worthy of particular attention. The use
of in-house publishing (or electronic publishing or desktop publishing) has seemingly opened a huge door to internal document
integration. The desire or need to produce attractive documents
runs the gamut in DP. Whether in word processing or technical
documents, organizations now realize the value of neat, attractive, and well-formed documentation.

They also realize the importance of maintaining control over
their own documentation. CDA would seem almost made to
order for this new philosophy. Desktop publishing obviously has
played a role in Digital's push to achieve this new standard. The
implementation of desktop publishing software and word processing software that has made it very easy for a user to create
text and graphics is clearly one of the driving forces in Digital's
push to address a total environment.

This networking issue also plays right along with current
methods of data processing that integrate (or attempt to inte-

grate) all facets of organizational activities. Desktop publishing has typically been associated with desktop solutions, but there haven't been many solutions to address the network perspective.

CDA is not so much a means to provide solutions to one particular area (like desktops or networks), but to provide a means to address solutions across all platforms. CDA was designed to be platform-independent and operating system-independent, according to Digital. CDA is designed as a universal interchange format that is independent of the desktop device or the operating system being used.

The object of CDA is to support all platforms considered a part of Digital's network application support strategy. That includes VT emulating PCs running MS-DOS and OS/2, Apple Macintoshes, and stand-alone workstations running under UNIX.

One of the unique features of CDA is its Live Links. Through this useful tool, all CDA compatible documents can be tied together so that they can be universally and simultaneously appended or updated. This means that when a change is made to a database or spreadsheet, for example, all associated documents will be automatically updated with the changed information.

The user has the option to turn off the Live Links at will should the document version need to be frozen for a time. This tool is invaluable to organizations with large data bases and DP operation in general. The worry of updating each element of associated material for a particular project is virtually eliminated. Live Links appears to be one of the most dynamically intriguing features of CDA, one that adds to an already intriguing proposition in standardization.

CHAPTER SUMMARY

At the broadest level, a computer is a computer is a computer. And today the general computer world seems to be moving closer to the ideal Digital has held for years. Tightly linked CPUs and distributed applications are becoming the norm, while work on communications standards worldwide is bringing the hardware and applications of all vendors closer together.

For Digital, DECnet not only forms the backbone of its communications but is an integral part of the company's overall philosophy for computer design. Through Digital and third-party products an increasing number of CPUs and applications can now work together over DECnet. When DECnet Phase V (DECnet/OSI) is fully operational in the early 1990s, network users can access common facilities using proprietary Digital protocols or OSI standard protocols.

Such moves are changing the face of computing from the end-user position all the way up to the mainframe.

CHAPTER 3

DECwindows

Too long minicomputer users have suffered with lackluster, plain-Jane user interfaces. Long after their PC and Macintosh counterparts enjoyed graphics, color, pull-down menus, icons, and all the rest, users of large systems were dealing with monochrome screens and scrolling menus.

The move is definitely on to a better day. With the example of the graphical Macintosh firmly placed as a goal to attain, minicomputer hardware and software designers are moving their products into the end-user mainstream (see Figure 3.1).

Digital is fully behind the industry trend toward more friendly user interfaces. DECwindows is the company's implementation of MIT's X Window System and, much as it has for the rest of the industry, the movement of X window technology into the Digital mainstream caused a revolution of sorts inside the company.

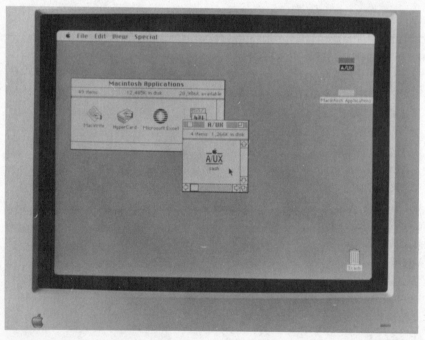

FIGURE 3.1 In the Apple Macintosh world, even the operating system is accessed through a graphical user interface that uses icons and menus. The X Window System and Digital's implementation, DECwindows, is providing similar facilities. [Courtesy of Apple Computer, Inc.]

The ultimate goal of the DECwindows development program is to make the DECwindows interface the standard for all of Digital's software offerings. That concept required some basic changes in the internal structure of the company.

Internally, Digital personnel have always been individuals competing with one another, according to a developer who worked on early DECwindows projects. The different departments—UNIX people, PC people, VMS people—have always been in competition with each other. DECwindows development was the first major program in the company that forced cooperation for success.

The level of cooperation required to produce DECwindows was unprecedented within Digital, developers say. VMS experts worked closely with UNIX/Ultrix people to refine the basic product to make it more portable across various platforms.

At the heart of DECwindows is the Digital user interface, XUI (Xwindow User Interface). Although Digital applications that use XUI have their own look and feel, the idea behind a standard such as DECwindows is to make the transition from one application to another easy for users and developers.

XUI is Digital's own implementation of a windowed user interface, but it is similar to the X Window System standard defined by MIT's Project Athena, an educational program funded jointly by Digital, IBM, and MIT. All of the major computer vendors have embraced the X Window System and are working on their own implementations of it. A movement by the Open Software Foundation is attempting to standardize windows-based user interfaces; other vendors are going their own way.

The result is slightly different user interfaces across workstation and minicomputer platforms. However, they all are similar to each other and, if the foundation laid by standards bodies holds, the logic interface to these systems will be easily accessible by software developers. Even as various systems evolve, the end-user benefits greatly from the graphics-oriented nature of new software that adheres to the X Window System standards.

Now, instead of having to learn how to access the features of each new software package, which is based on the individual design ideas of each company, you will understand immediately the basic features of every software package because of the common user interface.

In addition to presenting a consistent "window" into applications, DECwindows and other X Window System implementations provide other advantages. For example, with DECwindows-compliant applications you can run a program on the CPU of your choice across the network and display it on a different desktop device.

The windows environment also lets you conduct multiple operations simultaneously. Not only can you access applications and facilities through an easy-to-use icon-based screen (similar to the interface made popular by the Apple Macintosh computer), but you can open multiple windows. Each onscreen window acts like another terminal and you can run multiple local or remote applications together on the same screen.

You can start a long database sort or report on a networked cluster in one window, for example, then switch to another window to write your monthly report with an application running on your desktop workstation. Using X terminal hardware (see the following discussion) you can run these applications even if you don't have a workstation on your desk. Moreover, these networked applications can reside on UNIX/Ultrix or VMS systems.

Probably the most important aspect of X Window System technology, including DECwindows, is not the mild controversy that surrounds which presentation interface to use; rather, it is the fact that the underlying technology that makes the system work has been standardized. Figure 3.2 shows DECwindow components.

The protocols for linking applications to the X window environment have been in place for several years. Developers can safely use them to tie their products into this emerging standard. There hasn't been wholesale movement in this direction until recently, however, because of a number of factors.

For one thing, vendors were hesitant to make changes with the interface question unsettled. The real strength of a system like X Windows is its commonality, which enables users to move easily among applications without much retraining.

Further, such a system extracts a certain amount of overhead from the local and remote CPU. Until recently workstations powerful enough to support X windows with a reasonable amount of speed and power simply weren't available to a broad user base at affordable prices.

DECwindows Components

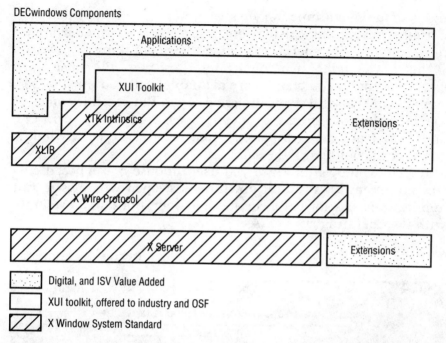

FIGURE 3.2 DECwindows components. The DECwindows system is Digital's implementation of the X Window System standard. DECwindows further defines a consistent look and feel for X-based applications, called XUI. XUI provides a style guide and programming library to assist developers in building sophisticated graphic-user interfaces with a consistent look and feel. [Reprinted with permission of Digital Equipment Corporation.]

These two factors are being resolved, and user awareness of window interfaces in general is heightened. Whereas a few years ago minicomputer and mainframe users were content with scrolling and lackluster presentation systems, many have now been exposed to PCs and Macintosh machines with bit-mapped graphics, color, and even motion video and sound. The days of new software with limited menuing systems are passing rapidly; X window interfaces and their derivatives are taking the place of conventional systems.

If you haven't personally been exposed to a desktop windowing interface, you will be soon. This is where the software industry is going to benefit all user classes.

In the past when you learned a new piece of software you had to find out which menu choices were available, what shortcuts or online help, if any, the programmer may have designed into the system, which function keys were active and what they did. Certain conventions existed, but there were no standards and most software designers were doing their own thing.

Under a standard windowing interface you still must learn which specific menu choices are available, and you must understand what the software is designed to do. But when it comes to making selections from that menu, or asking for help, printing, and other features, each package that adheres to the X window standards should work the same.

With a windows interface you use a mouse or keyboard cursor movement keys to pull down menus, open windows to run applications, ask for help, conduct file operations, and even talk with the operating system (see Figure 3.3).

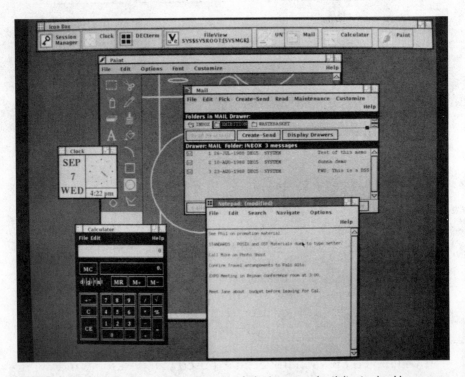

FIGURE 3.3 DECwindows offers a suite of desktop productivity tools. Users can work with various applications such as the clock, calculator, notepad, electronic mail, and paint programs on one screen. A consistent user interface across these built-in applications, as well as external applications written for DECwindows, reduces training and learning time. [Reprinted with permission of Digital Equipment Corporation.]

Once well established, such systems should shorten the training cycle for general system use and make the transition from application to application and from platform to platform much easier.

DECWINDOWS APPLICATIONS

DECwindows is now Digital's official front end for applications that are being shipped with VMS, and users of workstations, personal computers, and X terminals are benefiting from a standard look and feel on the screen.

Although not very many DECwindows-specific applications currently exist, software producers are working on them—either to convert existing software or to design new applications from scratch.

In the meantime, when you crack the box on DECwindows you'll find a number of ready-to-run, windows-compliant applications. Not only are they useful desktop utilities, but they show you some of the things you can expect from this new environment as more software is developed.

This set of "out-of-the-box" applications offers

Window Manager

Session Manager

FileView

Bookreader

Calculator

Calendar

Cardfiler

Clock

Digital Data Interchange Format (DDIF) Viewer

DECterm

Extensible VAX Editor (EVE)

Mail

Notepad

Paint

Puzzle

The Window Manager, Session Manager, and FileView applications help define the DECwindows environment, establishing the graphical user interface (GUI) and helping windows-compliant applications run. The rest of the software supplied with DECwindows makes up a package of extremely useful desktop utilities. You are likely to keep several of these running on your screen all of the time.

WINDOW MANAGER

The Window Manager is Digital's version of the X Window System manager that controls application windows. It sets up the title bar and icons for applications.

SESSION MANAGER

The Session Manager handles user login and logout, enables window customizing such as window colors and size, and conducts other housekeeping chores. The Session Manager and the Window Manager are transparent to the user. When they work you won't know they are there.

FILEVIEW

FileView is the "DECwindows shelf" or user executive. It gives you a way to look at all of your files and directories. You can use it to navigate around file directories and to do traditional operations on those files, such as comparing, saving, loading, and typing them. You can also use FileView to run applications against those files.

A setup routine lets you program FileView to customize the pop-up menus it provides with each file type. For example, when you highlight a DDIF file, the menu would be a long list, including graphics editing and printing. If you point to an ASCII file, the list of options would be much shorter. FileView provides the shell from which most other operations are conducted.

BOOKREADER

Bookreader is a text retrieval package that presents information on the screen as an electronic book. It has a table of contents and index, just like a regular book, but you can search these lists and jump directly to the information you want. That enables you to open the book anywhere, or start at the beginning and read to the end.

CALCULATOR

You are not alone in feeling the frustration that comes when you realize that your $20,000 workstation can't do something simple like add 2 and 2. With the DECwindows calculator in a pop-up window, your workstation can compete favorably with a $10 handheld calculator. Not only can it add 2 and 2, but it can take square roots, compute percentages, subtract, and multiply.

The software draws a calculator in the window that looks remarkably like the inexpensive one you may have in your briefcase or purse. You access its functions with the PFx and Pxx function keys.

CALENDAR

The out-of-the-box calendar is one of the slickest applications supplied with DECwindows. It offers enhancements over Digital's original CAL program application and includes more functionality and an extremely easy-to-use interface.

You can display calendar entries in day, month, or year format, but you are likely to use the month display most often. It shows the current month, the next month, today's appointments, and the current time. Appointment slots are set at half hour intervals, but you can change that to meet your own needs. You can move up and back by clicking on the "Next Day" or "Previous Day" boxes, and the Macintosh-like scroll bar on the side moves the hourly appointments up and down.

Calendar supports a variety of alarm settings ranging from one minute to 24 hours prior to an appointment. You can set up repeat entries to schedule regular events, such as a staff meeting on the second Monday of every month.

CARDFILER

You'll use Cardfiler a lot. This is a simple database you can use to track contact names, addresses, and phone numbers, product lists, references, and notes. You can create multiple card files so that the information in any given file is a tightly grouped collection of data.

You can even add graphics images, such as Paint program drawings, to index cards. Or you can store scanned images, such as photographs, with a name and address or product list.

This is not a sophisticated database, but it is a serviceable list manager that will probably become one of the Out of the Box applications you have on the screen most of the time.

CLOCK

What would you do without an onscreen clock? Here, finally, is a use for the 32-bit, high speed CPU you have under the hood of that desktop computer or workstation. It displays a digital or analog clock in 12- or 24-hour format, shows the current date, and has an alarm to tell you when to go to lunch.

DDIF VIEWER

DDIF is Digital's standard file format for compound documents that contain multiple elements, such as text and graphics. DDIF

Viewer lets you look at such files in a DECwindows window. You can also view ASCII files, but they are automatically converted to DDIF format before they are put on the screen.

DECTERM

When an application has not been written for DECwindows, the only way to use it in a windows environment is through a terminal emulation window. DECterm lets you open as many of these terminal windows as your screen size allows.

You can customize the DECterm window size and shape, and conduct other terminal setup functions such as terminal ID and 8- or 7-bit characters, for example.

EVE

The Extensible VAX Editor essentially is TPU for windows. It is compatible with EDT and WPS keypad editing commands.

You can view two or more files at once with EVE, and use cut and paste features to move information among the various files. EVE also supports keyboard macros and custom key definitions.

MAIL

Mail is a multiwindow application into your mail database. The first window is a directory of all your mail messages, and you can open up folders and look at the messages within those folders. If you click on a listed message, the text of the message is displayed in a separate window.

The multiwindow feature lets you read new mail without interrupting the message you are reading or writing. DECwindows mail also lets you search for messages by type or sending group, and you can reply in a block or individually. You can use the EVE editor—or the VMS editor of your choice—to edit mail messages.

NOTEPAD

The Notepad editor is an ASCII editor for simple lists and notes, or it can be used to create and edit program files. You can have more than one notepad window open at once and move text from one window to another.

PAINT

Use Paint to draw sketches, maps, or other illustrations. The program is supplied with some drawing tools, including boxes, ovals, paintbrushes, pens, and spray paint. Some sample images are also supplied to show you how to use the program for various illustrations.

Paint supports PostScript and Sixel printers. You can also use the DDIF files it creates in other applications that support the format.

PUZZLE

What do you do when you're put on hold or you're waiting for someone to answer the phone? Turn to your workstation and call up Puzzle. This is a video version of a puzzle with sliding numbered squares that are scrambled when you load the program. The object of this diversion feature is to arrange the squares in ascending order using the fewest possible moves.

These out-of-the-box applications show the power and utility of the DECwindows user interface. We will soon present a number of applications that use this standard either from a workstation or through one of the new low-priced X-compatible X Terminals devices that are also destined to become popular as DECwindows and X Window System products invade the marketplace.

X TERMINALS

The popularity of the X Window System user interface, embodied in DECwindows and other vendor offerings, is accompanied by an upsurge in the number of available desktop terminals that run as X window servers. Because these devices enable users to service applications from multiple hosts across a network, they provide another viable way to support VAX-to-VAX communications.

The X Window System was originally designed to reside on workstations, complete computers with powerful CPUs running UNIX or another full operating system. Stimulated by the friendly user interfaces in PC-based applications, users demanded better ways to access their host-based applications, and vendors responded with X terminal products.

At the heart of this terminal beats a powerful 32-bit processor, something like a Motorola 68020, for example, which is also the CPU in some Sun and other vendors' workstations. Many X terminals support 1 to 4 Mbytes of memory, run on powerful internal programs stored in ROM or downloaded from a host, and are attached directly to Ethernet.

Although some users believe "workstation" is a better term for this new generation terminal, the people who make them say they're not workstations because they can't run general applications; they can only run the X Window System server program. Also, the $1,000 to $3,000 price of these X terminals is inexpensive compared to the cost of a workstation. These terminals do provide the touch and feel of a workstation, however, and workstation users who transfer to an X terminal should be very comfortable with the move.

"X Stations" is a new term used by some vendors to describe the X terminal products. This term recognizes the power advantage X Terminals have over conventional ones. Figure 3.4 shows a Digital X Terminal.

Whatever you call them, X Window System-compatible display devices are fueling a new industry while providing more users with workstation-like interfaces to host applications. By today's standards, these network display stations generally have two unusual features. First, they typically attach directly to the network through an internal Ethernet adapter, rather than to a host via a terminal server or direct serial line. Second, they include the graphical user interface (GUI) associated with window-oriented systems, such as the Apple Macintosh, including a mouse for user input and point-and-shoot icons.

FIGURE 3.4 Digital and other vendors are developing high-end terminals that support X Window System protocols, providing a graphical user interface and application consistency to terminal users. [Reprinted with permission of Digital Equipment Corporation.]

Two GUI standards are vying for acceptance. The Open Software Foundation's (OSF) Motif is the result of work by nearly 150 OSF members worldwide. Motif is loosely based on Digital's XUI user interface technology and has a look and feel similar to Hewlett-Packard's windowing system. Sun's Open Look is backed by Sun and AT&T and is based on technology licensed from Xerox. Both GUIs provide a Macintosh-like user interface, but each has unique look-and-feel features.

So both Motif and Open Look appear destined for broad acceptance. Many software vendors are committed to supporting both standards; further, X terminal hardware should support both because of the underlying X Window System interface standard.

Another aspect of the X Window System is multitasking operations. Through a windowed interface, users can bring up multiple applications on the screen at once, start processes in various windows, and leave them to run by themselves while working with an interactive process in another window. By manipulating the screen with a mouse, the user can switch among the windows at will.

The X Window System consists of a server and a client that work together. Both client and server can be inside the same device, such as a workstation, or one can reside on a host and the other at the desktop. The client software usually resides at the host and the server at the desk. The DECwindows environment design is shown in Figure 3.5.

Notice the apparent contradiction in terminology. We normally think of a server as the remote computing resource for disk, file, or database management. In the X environment the server is part of the user display station and accepts input from application clients, displays client data on the screen, and sends keyboard and mouse information back to the client for

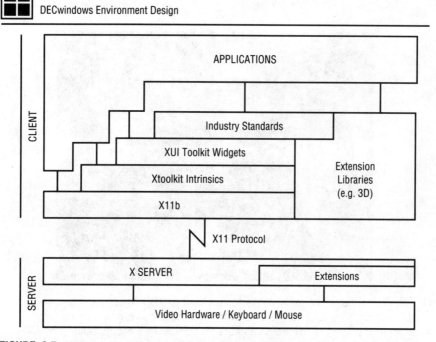

■■ DECwindows Environment Design

FIGURE 3.5 DECwindows environment design. The X Window system, on which DECwindows is based, consists of client and server components. [Reprinted with permission of Digital Equipment Corporation.]

processing. These individual resources can be shared among multiple applications, and the server software manages this interaction. In this context the term is appropriate and sensible.

Client software uses a graphics library (xlib) to send graphics requests to the server for processing and display, thereby enabling client-server compatibility even if they are implemented on different systems (see Figure 3.6). X-compatible software doesn't care what hardware platforms it uses and the hardware doesn't need to know where the software requests originate. Client-server communication occurs through X wire, a presentation protocol. As long as the standards are met at both ends of the link, the system works.

Some implementations, such as Digital's DECwindows, add enhancements to the basic architecture, but as long as the low-level components are compatible and the upper-level components are properly designed, compatibility can be maintained.

In addition to making it easier to run the same software on a variety of computers, X systems give the user a common inter-

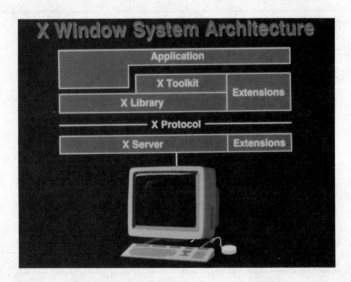

FIGURE 3.6 The X Window System architecture separates application-host and display-server components via a network interface. Basic graphics commands (in Xlib), interface tools, and extension libraries reside in the application host. The X server contains display-specific commands as well as translation tables that can support communications with different host-computer architectures. [Reprinted with permission of Digital Equipment Corporation.]

face for diverse applications including accounting, office automation, engineering, and communications. Eventually, as the standard becomes firmly established and more software is written to take advantage of X Window System features, the payback will be flexible software that uses the distributed features of today's networked systems and requires less training for end-users (see Figure 3.7).

The X Window System code can reside inside the terminal in ROM where it is instantly available when you turn the system on, or it can be downloaded from the host as part of the initial startup procedure. Most companies offer you either configuration though most recommend the host-based approach. This requires an extra step each time you bring a terminal up, but it permits

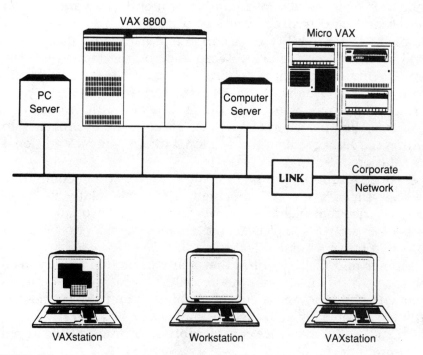

FIGURE 3.7 The X Window System permits workgroups, departments, and entire corporations to balance heterogeneous computers for optimum performance. With X, applications running in PC Server, Computer Server, VAX, and MicroVAX hosts can communicate via a corporate network with user-interface software in any X-compatible workstation or terminal. [Reprinted with permission of Digital Equipment Corporation.]

quick and easy upgrades when new software versions become available.

Applications software developers write applications to comply with the X standard rather than with specific terminals or computers, thereby providing a high degree of software portability across hardware platforms. In mid-1989 the X-compliant software available for these terminals was relatively limited. When X station hardware first appeared early in 1989, there was very little software written to take advantage of them.

By the end of 1989, however, the situation had changed, with software announcements occurring weekly. In addition to more X software, the range of available applications for technical and professional users expanded—word processing, graphics, CASE, and integrated office automation packages.

There are several reasons that new software is appearing more rapidly. It took developers a number of months to work through the research and writing processes after standards were firmly established. Availability of X-compliant hardware also stimulated software development. Acceptance by the industry of the two X Window System GUIs provided a sense of stability and comfortable environment for developers to work in.

No two companies ever do things in exactly the same way, of course, but in general there are three basic approaches to putting the X protocol on the desktop without using a traditional workstation.

As one solution, companies such as Network Computing Devices, Inc. are marketing a high-resolution, relatively large-screen device that includes a powerful CPU, a network interface, the server software in ROM, and enough memory to hold the fonts and other X-related features.

Another approach assumes that many users don't really need the full 1024 x 1024 resolution and high-speed processing common with X Window Systems. Acer Counterpoint approaches the problem by offering a 14-inch display with 640 x 480 resolution and an 8086 CPU at a price considerably below most full-featured X terminal devices.

A third solution is to run the server software on the host attached to the terminal and use the facilities onboard the terminal only for graphics processing. This results in reduced hardware and software requirements for the terminal—which lowers cost—but requires host-compatible software and computer re-sources. GraphOn takes this approach with its OptimaX 200 seri-al terminal. The terminal is priced in the low end of the range for X terminals and you have to buy one host license for the software.

By placing the server on the host the high overhead commu-nications don't have to travel over the serial link. In addition, GraphOn uses data compression for terminal communications to produce good interactive performance.

The technique also eliminates the need for an Ethernet inter-face at the terminal, and lowers terminal memory requirements, further reducing cost.

Each attached terminal requires its own host-based server, each running as a separate process on the VAX and consuming about 250 Kbytes of memory. However, the actual load on the host CPU is minimal, the company says.

There's a fourth solution that hasn't gotten much attention so far but which may become increasingly viable as end-user inter-est in X window systems rises. The approach is to simply run X-compatible software on a standard PC. Like the Acer solution, the PC approach provides lower graphics resolution and, except for high-end models, may exhibit relatively slow performance. But given the number of PC platforms already sitting on corporate desktops, it is a solution likely to meet with increased popularity.

Companies such as Locus Computing in California are intro-ducing PC-based software platforms to support the X windows environment. Their products run on all PC platforms from the basic 8088 machine through 80386s with lots of memory. The more powerful PC CPUs give better performance and can sup-port a wider array of operations, but it is encouraging to note the influx of host-compatible software that gives more users access to this environment.

Another positive development is a series of "desktop" software products that interface with the X environment to provide a finished end-user interface that can actually run programs from onscreen icons. The X Window standard by itself provides the GUI, but it is up to applications to make it work. Products such as X.Desktop from IXI Limited in England and Looking Glass from Visix in Arlington, VA, do just that.

IXI states its objective as making powerful computers easy to use so people who make powerful computers can sell them more widely, and users can use the power without being intimidated. X.Desktop puts a user interface shell on the computer, making it comfortable for more people.

NCR's Towerview terminal uses X.Desktop, and IXI believes such programs will be a strong influence in increasing the availability of UNIX—and the X terminal market–to more users.

Visix Software is specifically targeting the Macintosh user and others who want the graphical user-interface coupled with the power of workstations and UNIX hosts.

Stating that "the operating system interface is the classic thing holding up UNIX," Visix spent $6 million trying to solve the problem. The GUI standards make it possible for companies like these to enter the development market in a big way.

What will this influx of highly functional, relatively low-cost terminals mean to existing markets, such as workstations and very low-end terminals? That depends of whom you ask the question. Terminal manufacturers like Human Designed Systems in Philadelphia say the X terminal is just another product that fills in the gap between dumb terminals and workstations. Workstation producers like Hewlett-Packard say these new products are a way of giving more people access to the network with a user friendly device.

The people at Jupiter Systems in Alameda, CA, however, believe X terminals will start impacting the workstation market because they provide workstation-like performance at a lower cost and with less effort. Jupiter is marketing a $12,000, high-resolution color X terminal targeted at CADD, medical imaging, and other high-end applications. The Model 310's 68030 processor makes it among the fastest X terminals.

The influx of workstations has sometimes burdened professional staffs with the tasks of backup, maintenance, and other operations that were previously handled by a central MIS staff. With X station products that can give users the interface and easy access to applications they need, the industry may be returning, at least in part, to the old timesharing topology where the user didn't know and didn't care much about the device he or she was using.

Digital officials believe the low-end character terminal market "will stay pretty much flat" for the near term and that new X station hardware will not impact the workstation market, except perhaps in diskless workstations. In fact, if anything X terminal devices will improve workstation sales because customers can now feel comfortable putting workstations where they are really needed, Digital believes.

At least one workstation vendor, Sony Microsystems in San Jose, CA, believes the X terminal products will compete with low-end, diskless workstations but they cannot compete overall with workstations because of the additional load they extract on Ethernet.

Especially with X terminal products that download their operating code from the host, a large number of these products attached to a busy network could create a burden. With the rise in popularity of color and graphics terminals (we users never have enough. Once we get windowed, mouse-compatible interfaces, the next thing we demand is color and graphics displays) the communications demand of sending client (host) data to numerous X terminals, the increase in network traffic could have heavy impact.

Sony views X terminals as the 3270 or VT-100 of the future for applications where a 24 x 80 character display is not enough. Engineers and heavy users will still require desktop workstation power while X stations will improve application access for secretarial or even management query operations. Right now this prediction seems premature because of the wide price difference between workstations and X terminals. As the price of truly functional workstations declines, however, Sony's scenario becomes more realistic.

Sony's $3,000 NWS-711 diskless workstation and similar products could be viable alternatives to X terminals because they provide local processing, offloading some of the network traffic. However, market demand will lead Sony and other reluctant vendors into the X terminal arena. As with any new technology, a bit of "shake out" must occur before the impact on the industry can be precisely determined.

In addition to more products in the marketplace, we're seeing additional functionality included in the basic terminal box. Most systems support thick- and thin-wire Ethernet; some have twisted pair capability. Spectragraphics, which is marketing a terminal from NCR, includes IBM 3270 compatibility and hints that other similar onboard applications will soon be available.

The basic drive behind X terminals development is the appeal of high performance and low cost per user. In addition, the establishment of the Motif and Open Look display standards has ignited the software development community.

It is unlikely that X terminals will replace low-end terminals or workstations at the high-end. These devices appeal to specific audiences that need their special capabilities. But for the user who needs the power of UNIX or VMS with the ease of use of a PC and the low cost of a terminal, X terminals have a great deal of appeal.

CHAPTER SUMMARY

An integral part of the Digital computing environment is the DECwindows user interface. By adhering to standards based on the X Window System, Digital and other vendors are working together to ease the chore of learning new software, both systems and applications.

In addition, new developments such as X Window terminals that can provide near-workstation functionality at a fraction of the cost of a full workstation, will provide this desktop environment to nearly every VAX user over the next few years.

Such new developments not only make accessing the local host easier, but their support for distributed processing also makes everything on the network available to more users.

CHAPTER **4**

Networking
in the VAX
Environment

THE DIGITAL PHILOSOPHY
TECHNOLOGY OF VAX-TO-VAX NETWORK COMMUNICATIONS
OSI
DIGITAL AND OSI
PROTOCOLS
DECNET
OSI NETWORK LAYERS
   PHYSICAL LAYER
   DATA LINK LAYER
   NETWORK LAYER
   TRANSPORT LAYER
   SESSION LAYER
   PRESENTATION LAYER
   APPLICATION LAYER
DECNET NETWORK MANAGEMENT FEATURES
NETWORK MAINTENANCE
ADDITIONAL NETWORK STANDARDS
CHAPTER SUMMARY

Networking—connecting multiple computer platforms to share disk storage, printers, or computing power—was once a luxury reserved for only the very largest computing installations. Today the concept is widely accepted and the hardware and software required to implement local- and wide-area links is readily available.

For Digital Equipment Corporation, networking is an especially important part of corporate and marketing philosophy. Digital has one of the largest networks in the world. It is part of corporate culture, linking employees and departments in a global enterprise. The ability of any employee to reach almost any other employee across the network builds community and enables teams comprised of employees separated by half a world to work together on projects. Figure 4.1 shows the DECnet Open System Interconnection (OSI) Network.

And, of course, this corporate network enhances the computer power available for any given task. Work groups and departments have the processors they need close at hand, but they share CPUs and data from around the enterprise as necessary.

THE DIGITAL PHILOSOPHY

Distributed processing is the basis of Digital's computing philosophy. The network and its support components are all part of a computing whole that is used within the company and promoted to customers as part of the Digital VAX package.

Why distribute processing power? A number of advantages are possible, including:

Users share the organization's total computing power by exchanging information and through CPU use.

Information flows more freely throughout a networked organization. Networked users share corporate data, applications software, and the knowledge and expertise each user brings to the network.

Overall computing power is increased. Obviously, five or a dozen or a score of computers working together can do more

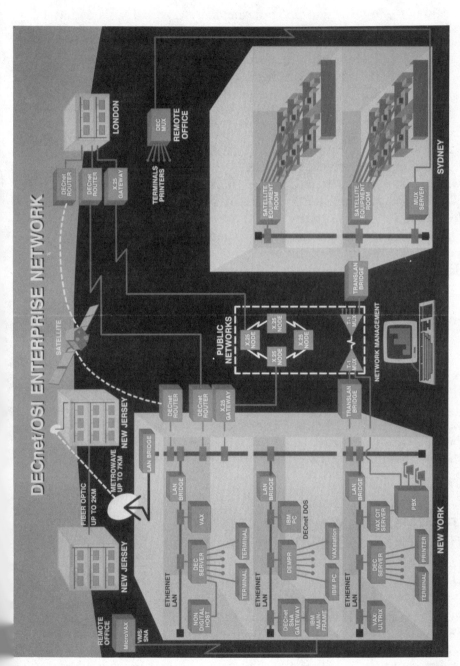

FIGURE 4.1 DECnet OSI Enterprise Network. Digital's own internal network reaches into virtually every corner of the globe, using more than 45,000 nodes. [Reprinted with permission of Digital Equipment Corporation.]

49

than a single machine, but they also form a whole that is more powerful than its individual parts working alone.

The network can allow each user or user group to select the equipment and software needed for specific tasks—even from a vendor different than one used by the rest of the organization—and still share facilities.

Digital's corporate networking philosophy, and the resulting Digital Network Architecture (DNA), grew from the company's own need to bring together the many systems it had created by the mid-1970s. There were so many different computing platforms in the company at that time that various segments were having difficulty sharing information and processing power. Out of this intra-company need grew DNA, encompassing DECnet, and a strengthening philosophy of interconnection and distributed processing began its evolution.

Over the years Digital has developed products that support resource sharing in a multicomputer environment through DECnet and other facilities. The list includes clustering hardware and software; gateways to Cray, IBM, and other specific foreign architectures; and direct and local area network (LAN) links to personal computers. Digital's stated philosophy is to provide users with the tools and techniques required for multivendor communication, a goal they have approached by supporting international communications guidelines while maintaining compatibility with their own standards.

TECHNOLOGY OF VAX-TO-VAX NETWORK COMMUNICATIONS

Ethernet forms the backbone of Digital networking. The Ethernet standard has been adopted for LAN applications by virtually every computer vendor. In fact, Digital estimates that over half of the installed LANs worldwide use Ethernet. The standards-setting work of the Institute of Electrical and Electronics Engineers (IEEE) has helped provide Ethernet links to users of about any computer vendor's hardware. The IEEE 802.3

standard specifies how information is exchanged over Ethernet. The standard does not specify how this information will be interpreted. That is up to individual host hardware and software.

Ethernet can transfer data among attached devices at up to 10 megabits per second (Mbps), about one million characters per second. The actual rate of exchange is less than this because of network overhead required to sort out messages from different users, route them properly, and handle conflicts that occur when two devices try to send messages at the same time.

Direct Ethernet links operate to about 4,000 feet, depending on the medium used to carry the traffic and other hardware that may be present on the network. You can connect multiple networks to extend Ethernet's working distance. Digital calls this configuration "Extended Ethernet."

Ten Mbps DECnet Ethernet is the basic standard for Digital LANs. Other international standards are broadening the appeal of Ethernet by establishing rules for communicating, including how each host interprets network data and how each information presents information to the user.

OSI

Open System Interconnection (OSI) is the international model for linking computer systems from different vendors. OSI is the product of a standards committee of the Geneva-based International Standards Organization. The American ISO representative is ANSI, the American National Standards Institute.

OSI was founded in the 1970s. Digital and IBM were already developing their own networking standards at the time. For Digital it was DNA; IBM's version was SNA, System Network Architecture. Figure 4.2 shows the Enterprise Network Environment OSI backbone.

IBM and Digital—along with all major businesses in the minicomputer marketplace—are embracing OSI standards. Digital has made more progress in this area than many vendors because of the company's early experience (and problems) in linking their own incompatible systems and because of their long-standing commitment to networking.

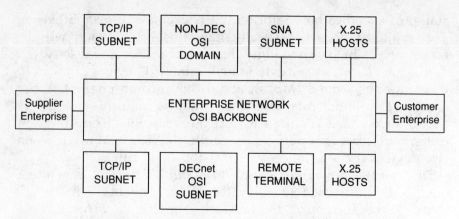

FIGURE 4.2 Enterprise Network Environment OSI Backbone. By starting with an OSI-standard backbone, Digital networking can reach a wide variety of hosts and other systems. [Reprinted with permission of Digital Equipment Corporation.]

DIGITAL AND OSI

Digital's OSI strategy is to have it both ways. The company has promised to maintain the current, proprietary DECnet protocols as it moves to OSI compliance. This approach provides continuing support for existing users, while laying an OSI-compliant architecture on top of it.

With DECnet/OSI (DECnet Phase V), applications can choose which communications protocol to use in any given situation. For Digital-to-Digital communications, DECnet protocols are probably the best choice because they are faster, the company claims, and they have more features. When information is routed into a multivendor environment, OSI protocols should be selected. Digital claims this simultaneous compliance with the two standards is the best way to support existing and future applications.

PROTOCOLS

OSI describes a seven-layer architecture in which each layer conducts separate but related functions (see Figure 4.3). Higher

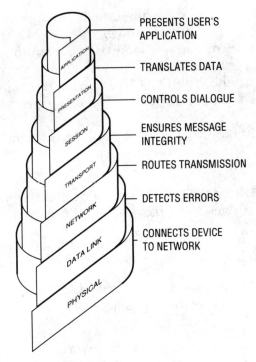

PRESENTS USER'S APPLICATION

TRANSLATES DATA

CONTROLS DIALOGUE

ENSURES MESSAGE INTEGRITY

ROUTES TRANSMISSION

DETECTS ERRORS

CONNECTS DEVICE TO NETWORK

APPLICATION

PRESENTATION

SESSION

TRANSPORT

NETWORK

DATA LINK

PHYSICAL

FIGURE 4.3 Open Systems Interconnect model. The seven-layer approach permits changes to individual levels without affecting the entire model. Vendors who adhere to the standard can theoretically integrate their systems easily. [Reprinted with permission of Digital Equipment Corporation.]

layers use the layers below them, but the details of how the lower layers do what they do are transparent to higher layers. The modular design permits changes or even significant redesign of any module without affecting associated modules, as long as the basic functionality and inter-layer communication are maintained.

Key elements of a protocol are syntax, semantics, and timing. Syntax specifies signal levels and data formats. Semantics supports coordination among machines and data handling. Timing matches communication speeds and sequences data packets if they arrive out of order.

The OSI protocol specifies precisely how information is exchanged across a network. OSI standards groups have spent more than ten years hammering out the details of the protocol, and the basic seven layers are now firmly established and agreed to by various international standards organizations.

Although confirming additional areas of protocol could take ten more years, the stability of the basic seven layers enables hardware and software vendors to develop products based on the standard.

The approximate breakdown of OSI layer functions is as follows:

1–3 Defines the physical aspects of connectivity: wiring and cables, data encoding, addressing, and data management.

4–6 Provides interoperability among different systems: session control, dialog management, and format conversion.

7 Handles distributed applications: file transfer, remote file access, and database management.

Names and functions of the seven layers are presented in the following list.

Layer	Name	Function
7	Application	Presents User Applications
6	Presentation	Translates Data
5	Session	Controls Dialogue
4	Transport	Ensures Message Integrity
3	Network	Routes Transmissions
2	Data Link	Detects Errors
1	Physical	Connects Network Devices

Although Digital has stated its commitment to OSI standards, as with other standards already in wide use, some of the terminology and the actual implementation have unique elements. DNA, which includes DECnet, is loosely grouped into three levels: link, management, and application.

Link Layer	Supervises communications hardware and message packetization. For point-to-point connections in an all-Digital system, DECnet creates packets, transmits them, and decodes them using the Digital Data Communications Message Protocol (DDCMP). In a heterogeneous environment, DNA's link layer could be replaced by Ethernet or X.25 communications.
Management Layer	Supervises message routing among DECnet nodes by calculating the lowest-cost route for a particular message from among the various physical links available. DECnet can find alternate paths if individual lines or network nodes fail. This feature is called "adaptive routing capability."
Application Layer	Supports message and data interchange among programs running on different nodes of the network. Similar to IBM's LU 6.2, this facility supports networked applications such as shared data bases and electronic mail.

Applications use the first four layers of DECnet/OSI (Phase V) just as they would in any OSI network. After the fourth layer, applications can decide whether to use the OSI stack or Digital's proprietary protocols. In this way, existing applications are not hampered by the switch to OSI standards, and new OSI-compliant applications should function satisfactorily. In addition, designers can use the proprietary parts of DNA if they consider it a better choice for a given application.

DECNET

DECnet is an important part of the Digital product line which originated as an internal communications tool in 1974. Although it predates work on OSI networking by about five years, many of the original DECnet concepts are embodied in OSI.

Digital expanded its interconnection philosophy to include multivendor environments in parallel with a worldwide push for computer communications standards during the mid- and late-1980's. Although still committed to some proprietary features, such as the VMS operating system, Digital has officially recognized the need for easy integration of computer hardware and software from multiple vendors.

DECnet is software that runs with Ethernet. By convention, however, the term "DECnet" usually means the Ethernet hardware and software as well as the additional DECnet software. DECnet software is a part of Digital's operating systems, providing network communications features to all of the company's computer systems.

Digital's Network Architecture has undergone a number of revisions over the years. Phase V (DECnet/OSI) is the latest version, and it adheres closely to the OSI model while maintaining proprietary features Digital views as essential for maximum functionality. With the introduction of Phase V in 1987, Digital established a three-year program for providing full OSI compliance.

DECnet and OSI are similar, parallel, and simultaneous architectures. Ultimately, DECnet will be smart enough to understand which protocol stack any applications software is using, and network access calls will be automatically routed over OSI or DECnet.

Among Digital's stated design goals for DNA are:

Transparent operation. Network access should be invisible and simple. From the Digital management perspective, the network should require a minimum of intervention.

Broad-based and flexible support for technologies and applications. DNA can handle a wide range of applications, communications facilities, and network topologies. The Digital system is being designed to handle communication of voice, data, and images throughout an enterprise. The Digital "network vision" for the future is "to communicate anything, to anywhere, at anytime."

In addition, DNA is designed to permit growth, to support migration to new architectures, and to be implemented in stages or subsets for installations that don't need all of its features. The simplest DECnet installation is two nodes, but that small beginning can be expanded to as many as 64,000 nodes with Phase IV DECnet. For all practical purposes, under Phase V the number of nodes is unlimited.

Standards support. Digital supported the OSI standard from the beginning and has been instrumental in helping to evolve the specifics of OSI recommendations.

Decentralized and secure facilities. Distributed computing is one of Digital's basic philosophies. Many DNA features, such as routing and network management, are not centralized. Decentralization is an important factor in maintaining high availability (reliability) and security. Specific security features are also built into DNA.

OSI NETWORK LAYERS

There will be some slight differences between OSI and DNA through the 1990s and beyond. Basically, however, DECnet Phase V *is* an OSI network with seven compatible layers. A discussion of the various OSI network layers is presented.

PHYSICAL LAYER

This layer consists of wiring, cables, and fiber optics. It handles such mundane tasks as converting computer-level data into electrical signals that can be sent across the network, and back again on the other end. Standards specify plugs, connectors, sockets, and other physical aspects of interconnection. The physical layer carries the network signals. In addition to mechanical specifications, this layer covers encoding techniques and modulation standards. Other functions include monitoring communications channels and managing the physical layer connections (dialup lines, X.21, and so forth).

DATA LINK LAYER

This layer contains data packets and intersystem communications. It controls the data stream from one system to another. The data link layer ensures error-free communications across the network through communications protocols that detect and correct data errors originating in the physical layer. Protocols include Advanced Data Communications Control Procedures (ADCCP), bisynchronous and high-level data link control (HDLC), CCITT X.25 for packet-switched network communications, and the IEEE 802.3 local area network standard. This layer supervises assembly of data packets, checks sent data, sends "message received" to the sending node, and resends data when an error message is received.

NETWORK LAYER

The network layer handles data packet addressing and message routing. It selects the physical pathway between nodes, choosing either a fixed route or one based on network conditions, priorities of service, or other situations. The database and interpreting logic of the network layer can support hundreds of thousands of nodes. The location of the network layer varies greatly with the design of the network; in a common carrier network or other major trunk network, network layer functions are typically provided by an external controller.

TRANSPORT LAYER

This layer is concerned with data integrity. It takes over where the network layer leaves off. The transfer layer performs network-layer-type functions at the local level, and controls the information flow between nodes once the path is established, maximizes network resources by managing network use to avoid congestion, matches send-receive transmission rates, and retransmits undelivered packets. If the network fails, the transport layer software searches out alternate routes or finds a way to save transmitted data until the network connection is re-established.

One of the protocols of the transport layer is the Transmission Control Protocol, part of the TCP/IP package.

SESSION LAYER

This layer handles dialog control, application communication, security, and housekeeping. It selects the proper communications protocol between users, manages transport-layer connections, and enforces access control policies. The session layer supervises security, passwords, and logging on/off. These OSI layers carry data further up the line toward an application, providing interfaces between the application and the network. The session layer manages the logical connections between network users and applications, and begins the proprietary portion of DECnet.

PRESENTATION LAYER

This layer is concerned with data translation and application look and feel. The presentation layer determines control codes, character sets, graphics characters, and commands that give programs their distinctive look. It smooths out differences among multivendor systems by converting (translating) information among nodes to maintain a consistent presentation.

APPLICATION LAYER

This layer handles the user interface. It contains the network operating system and applications programs, including electronic mail, file sharing, and data bases.

DECNET NETWORK MANAGEMENT FEATURES

Imagine a darkened room lit only by a multicolored wall of CRTs higher than your head and as wide as a barn. The computer-driven displays show lists of cities and node names, performance data, error messages, action notices, and world and regional maps with cities and buildings connected by colored lines.

Looking more like a spaceship bridge than anything earthly, this display is, in fact, the manager's position of a global computer network. The developments for totally automated, "lights out" network management aren't in place, but that is the direction of the industry.

Nearly all network products have some level of network management built in. Standards under OSI allow disparate network hardware to communicate data about current status and operating conditions, to promote standardized user interfaces, and to develop common database and reporting specifications.

With an increasing number of computer users sharing data and other facilities over networks, network management becomes more important. Network management serves two primary purposes. It supports design, implementation, and control of network performance and manages network changes.

The management of even a small network includes the following functions:

- Maintains user network access

- Provides security facilities such as passwords and other structures and procedures to ensure data integrity.

- Monitors network activity and tunes for maximum efficiency

- Detects and corrects operational and procedural problems

- Organizes network data into useful statistics to aid in planning for growth

The ISO/OSI Management Framework groups network management functions into five basic areas: configuration, fault, performance, accounting, and security.

One useful aspect of DECnet is the number of network management tools it has built in. Digital markets optional network monitoring and management hardware and software, but the basic network can handle day-to-day operations such as automatically adjusting to changes in the system and bypassing failed components.

With very large networks it can be difficult to find where problems exist and to identify what is causing them. As users and facilities are added, portions of the network can slow down for a number of reasons including inefficient software, inappropriate network activities by one or more users, or equipment problems.

Processes such as updating user access rights, adding software, adding or removing a user, changing network configuration, and data backup become complicated and time-consuming. Proper tools and procedures make these tasks more manageable.

Network efficiency is important. Monitoring traffic, identifying different types of network activities, detecting differences in speed across various network segments, and storing data for later analysis all help identify and correct problems.

Network management can be a full time job for one or more employees depending on the number of network users. Digital promotes the efficiency of DECnet and its management tools which allow a minimum number of people to handle the management functions. When Digital's internal network supported only 2,000 nodes worldwide, for example, there were six full-time network management people. In 1989 with a network over 15 times as large, the number of network management personnel has grown to only 18, three times as many.

A network is managed by people who use information collected from a number of resources to detect problems, to tune network operation, and to plan for future operations. They use networked hardware and software resources to support these tasks. Software such as DECnet has some built-in network management facilities. Additionally, other software tools for data collection and analysis can be added.

Network managers access the network through a terminal or workstation that has access to the management software and other facilities that help them do their job. The managers can display real time usage information about the network, design and print reports, conduct statistical analysis on the data, produce graphs and charts, and even disable and enable network functions from the manager's workstation or terminal. Figure 4.4 shows a basic management system.

Obviously the manager does not have to sit in front of a screen all day watching network events to find out about the operation of the system. Usually there are monitoring tools—either dedicated hardware that is a separate network node or software that

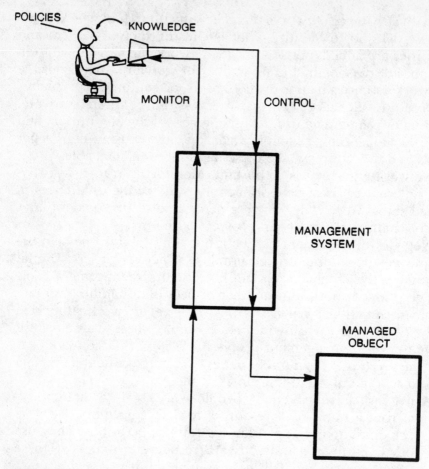

FIGURE 4.4 A management system provides access to objects in a network and supports functions that monitor and control the object. In Digital's model, a user performs management operations based on policies that are set by the user's organization. Policies set constraints and thresholds and define levels of service the object must provide to the enterprise. Objects can include anything from processors and applications to the communication devices that link them. Policies define network criteria, such as the level of access to and availability of applications, the required performance and throughput of links, and other issues of concern to the management organization. [Reprinted with permission of Digital Equipment Corporation.]

runs on one of the network's CPUs—that capture operational data throughout a day or other period (see, for example, Figure 4.5). The manager can then display statistics at any time, compare the current statistics against those for previous periods, and project facility requirements into the future.

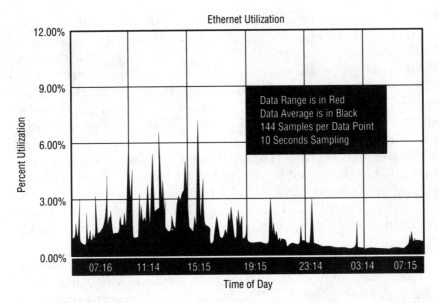

FIGURE 4.5 Software tools, such as Digital's LAN Traffic Monitor, can provide continuous and long-term analysis of network conditions, including utilization and throughput data. [Reprinted with permission of Digital Equipment Corporation.]

As hardware and software tools evolve, the breadth and scope of these basic tools will change. For example, configuration management today generally includes the ability to set up and change operating parameters of the network and to identify network components. Future expert systems will probably be able to conduct a great deal of the planning required to establish or expand a network. In addition, fault management, already fairly sophisticated, will provide more predictive functions capable of correcting a problem before network users become aware of it.

The evolving standardized user interface will also enhance network management. Digital already has a number of graphics display elements in operation that inform management personnel of network status and performance problems, loads, and faults. As you view a world map of network links, for example, green lines mean everything is working normally. You may see a link turn amber if the system senses an impending problem, indicated, for example, by a rise in segment usage or fall in performance. A downed link may be shown in red.

As such tools become standard and more sophisticated, the job of the network manager may change in the same way the duties of an airline pilot have changed in the last half century. No longer does the pilot of a large airliner personally manipulate the controls over every mile of the flight. Rather, sophisticated computers help plot the route, monitor systems, report problems, and fly the plane. The pilot handles takeoffs and landings directly and steps in to solve problems. The job description of the network manager is tending toward this same type of intelligent, highly trained overseer.

With DECnet Phase V, Digital added a network control language (NCL), which makes it easier to control other network management features. NCL provides authorized personnel access to the management directives (commands issued to control or monitor network components) that are defined for all network components.

The Phase V DNA model also includes an ISO-compliant Common Management Information Protocol (CMIP) that runs at the application layer. CMIP is a request-response protocol that enables managers to get and set management attributes, to request execution of management actions, and to report various network events.

The basic structure for network management under OSI consists of several pieces:

- Repository, a data base of network-wide management information

- Executive, an operating system for the management system

- Interface

- Presentation Module

- Access Module

Digital employs a scheme called EMA (Enterprise Management Architecture) on DECnet. Digital defines EMA as "a framework for the management of heterogeneous, multivendor distributed computing environments and the communications facilities that link them. It is a highly flexible architecture designed to enable network and system operations personnel to design and implement environments to meet their specific organizational and technical requirements."

Digital views compatibility across applications and hardware platforms as essential. Moreover, Digital's strategy treats network management as only one part of overall enterprise management that includes even applications and user interfaces.

The major network players, including Digital, are settling into an OSI-compliant posture for network management as well as other facets of networked communications. One major component of this architecture is the protocol through which distributed network components communicate.

Under OSI's distributed architecture it will be increasingly important for networked devices, including bridges, routers, and multiplexers, for example, to know about each other and to report to a common management facility in a standard way. The natural evolution of the network will lead to increasingly intelligent devices, enabling previously low-level devices to become part of the peer-to-peer relationship.

OSI calls for two general classes of device, directors and entities. An entity is anything being managed and a director is something that does the management. An entity is any object that can support a minimum level of management operations, including network nodes, LAN bridges, packet data network switches, modems, and even applications.

A director is a software system that provides the interface between human or other software management system users and the entities that they control and monitor.

Even as industry-wide developments move toward OSI, communications companies must provide network management solutions that work today and that can grow into OSI compatibility in the future. Digital's DECnet architecture has some migration facilities built into the basic design.

The key to long-term interoperability is to get OSI's CMIP-compatibility in all environments. Another protocol, CMOT (CMIP on TCP/IP) will accomplish this transition to the advanced network performance features that will support networked users well into the next decade. The interim CMOT protocol can move through current standards to the ultimate goal.

With versions of CMIP on all types of networks, better device-independence is achieved, an increasingly important requirement with larger, more diverse networks.

Digital identifies three levels of network management: automatic management, semi-automatic management, and manual management. Management systems are provided in Figures 4.6 and 4.7.

Automatic management can be conducted inside individual networked components. A bridge, for example, may maintain its own configuration table that includes information about the connections it is servicing. A remote director can query the bridge, using the CMIP protocol, to download that data. Intelligent bridges and routers can even change network routing in response to changing load requirements or to handle system faults.

Semi-automatic management involves devices that report to a central management system when conditions change or an error occurs. The managed device can supply unsolicited data to its

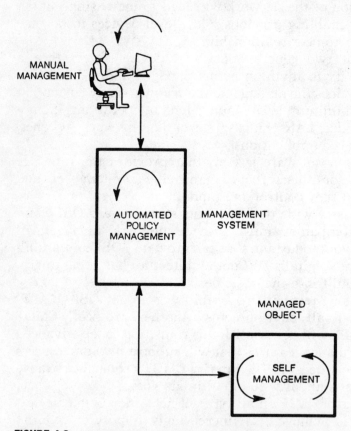

FIGURE 4.6 With increasingly intelligent network entities, many devices contain self-management capabilities that interface with other management tools on the network. [Reprinted with permission of Digital Equipment Corporation.]

FIGURE 4.7 Network management systems, such as the ACS 4800 from Advanced Computer Communications, provide sophisticated, graphics-oriented displays. [Reprinted with permission of Advanced Computer Communications.]

director, but the director makes decisions about what to do with that information.

At the highest level is the human network manager who makes basic policy decisions, or changes configurations that are beyond the scope of the intelligent devices on the network. These human decisions are based on input from distributed devices and are influenced by the reporting and analysis software that is part of the management environment.

In a time of change and growing network management importance, Digital suggests these steps to help users establish a baseline management system:

- Create a network management workstation with a node name that everybody knows, such as NETMANAGER.

- Establish an electronic mail account for users to mail notes about their problems.

- Provide a bulletin board-type device where users can comment about the network.

- Publish a weekly notice that includes a network census, new sites that have come on the network, and policy changes.

- Implement a security policy that users read and agree to before they join the network. This provides a common initial level of network security.

These simple procedures help any management system, from the simplest to the most complex. They form a foundation on which you can build automated, expert systems, but they also enhance the management scheme of the most basic LAN. Coupled with enough foresight to predict how growing user requirements and advanced technology will affect your future networking needs, these steps might make the transition into the future an easier one.

NETWORK MAINTENANCE

Digital Equipment Corporation's strong presence in the networking field and their work with DECnet and OSI is well known. Perhaps less visible are Digital's efforts in network maintenance at customer sites. In fact, a separate network services group within the field service division regularly conducts sophisticated studies and analyses of network installations to help customers plan networks, to isolate and correct problems, and to predict potential networking difficulties.

The group offers the following five levels or elements of service:

- Maintenance planning
- Configuration management
- Fault management, the expertise to dial in and identify network faults
- Fault resolution management
- Predictive maintenance

The service itself is interesting, but one of the most intriguing aspects of the service is the Digital Service Processor (DSP), a specially-configured MicroVAX II installed at a customer site by the network services group. The DSP sits on the customer network, monitoring its operation, storing data, and feeding information back to appropriate Digital field service locations.

Proprietary AI (artificial intelligence) tools on the DSP and at other Digital locations are an integral aspect of the system and enable effective preventive maintenance.

Digital's position is that the more critical the network becomes to the functioning of your organization, the more you need fault prevention. Traditional remedial service with minimal downtime is no longer adequate. Maximum network availability and, ideally, uninterrupted operation are the new criteria of effective service.

As part of the predictive maintenance service provided in cooperation with customers, Digital can periodically dial into the Digital Service Processor and use the network to look for developing faults. After gathering data, the company makes recommendations to correct developing problems before they take the network down.

The MicroVAX is enhanced with a common interface to several software packages to make the service easier to maintain. Included with the software resident on the DSP platform are the following features:

LTM (LAN Traffic Monitor)

Remote network manager

Configuration management data base

The original concept emphasized maintenance management, but the service seems to be evolving toward additional network management services.

The DSP is tied back to Digital's customer support centers, which supply some AI tools to study the data collected in the field. By calling the center for assistance, a service customer has access to a service team.

The typical member on this team has between 10 and 15 years of hardware and software experience and has been trained to analyze problems in a network environment, the company reports. Digital sees the maintenance organization as an extension of the existing customer support staff, in providing both technical capability and network expertise.

Who are the customers for such high-tech services? One might first assume that they are companies with hundreds of network nodes and complicated systems. Not so, according to digital service representatives, who say Digital has customers using the DSP and associated services with as little as one network node. They simply don't have the in-house expertise required to manage their own system and are running applications that depend heavily on network communications.

Another potential set of users are customers in the distributed world who need some support to help ease the transition into this very rapidly changing technology. The ideal for them is probably to be able to handle such services in-house with support from the vendor as required. However, if your networking facilities are growing rapidly and you don't have the financial resources required to hire the expertise or you need help during the transition, Digital field service offerings could be worthwhile.

ADDITIONAL NETWORK STANDARDS

In addition to the standards already discussed under DECnet, a number of specific standard specifications may be involved in establishing a network. These specific standards evolved with OSI development or they served as guidelines when the OSI standards were defined.

The Institute of Electrical and Electronics Engineers (IEEE), for example, has published a set of standards for the two lowest levels of the OSI model. These definitions include cabling, electrical, and physical design.

IEEE 802.3 (also known as ISO 8802.3) is closely related to Ethernet schemes from Digital Equipment Corporation, Xerox, 3Com, and others. 802.3 is a data link layer standard that controls how information is passed over a network. It is based on Ethernet Carrier Sense Multiple Access/Collision Detect (CSMA/CD) technology.

IEEE 802.5 (ISO 8802.5) defines a "Token-Ring" architecture like that used by IBM. A logical token is circulated around a physical ring topology, and handed off to the node that requests it in turn. The node that possesses the token is given exclusive access to the network.

IEEE 802.4 (ISO 8802.4) is also a token-passing architecture, but the physical arrangement is a bus. The 802.4 networks function as a logical ring.

The International Telephone and Telegraph Consultative Committee (CCITT) has also originated standards that have been adopted by many hardware and software vendors around the world.

The CCITT X.25 protocol, for example, establishes methodologies for communicating across packet switched data networks (PSDN). Like the IEEE 802.x specifications, X.25 is a low-level protocol. Interpretation of the information exchanged over an X.25 network must be handled by individual applications.

X.400 is important because it establishes standards for electronic mail interchange, and because it is the first higher-layer application available under OSI. The standard specifies how private mail systems and public carriers will transfer mail messages internally and between private and public systems, and it specifies store-and-forward mail service. X.400 was established as a mail system standard in 1984, prompting a number of companies to introduce products based on it. Digital's MailBus is one example of an X.400-compliant product.

File transfer access and management standards (FTAM) handle the actual control of file transfers between systems at the application layer. FTAM standards were finalized in 1988 and will provide methodologies for file exchange among multivendor systems.

Other application layer standards include virtual terminal protocol (VTP), common application service elements (CASE), and job transfer and manipulation. These standards further enhance your ability to connect products from multiple vendors successfully in a network.

CHAPTER SUMMARY

This chapter is designed to introduce most of the basic concepts associated with networking in the Digital environment. The discussion is slanted toward DECnet, which is the primary Digital-related communications environment. But because DECnet is similar to the OSI model, the same concepts apply to networking products from many other vendors who are following these international standards.

Use this chapter as reference material for some of the terms and concepts associated with Digital networking. Other sections provide more details on issues like selecting network products and network configuration, for example.

How Do You Connect?

In the previous chapters we discussed the VAX computing environment and networking in general. In this section we offer an overview of the physical methods for connecting computers, with some technical background for each type of connection.

Consider this an introduction only. It should, however, provide enough detail to help you configure a VAX system and get a general idea of what you'll need for wiring and other hardware.

Of course you can exchange information among various computer systems by simply carrying a tape, removable hard disk, or floppy diskette from one machine to another. This slow and limiting method of data interchange, sometimes called "sneaker net," isn't practical when a large number of users need to share data over a wide physical area, or when the machines involved are incompatible.

It can work for occasional transfer of files or when the amount of data exchanged is so great that it would tie up a network for an unreasonable amount of time.

For smaller amounts of data, for ongoing communications, and for connecting computers that are located physically far apart from each other, you need a better solution.

Among the common links that connect VAXs are Ethernet running over various media, VAX clusters, and serial communications. We will discuss each of these connectivity solutions in this chapter.

VAX CLUSTERS

A cluster is a group of two or more computers connected to each other and to common storage devices through a high-speed parallel bus. Clustering allows multiple processors to work together on some applications, and it lets more than one host access high-capacity storage (see Figure 5.1).

The VAXcluster system was introduced in 1983, broadening the capabilities of distributed processing. VAXclusters allow computer systems to grow beyond a single CPU without replacing existing equipment.

Part of the cluster system involves extensions to the VMS operating system to support resource sharing such as disks, printers,

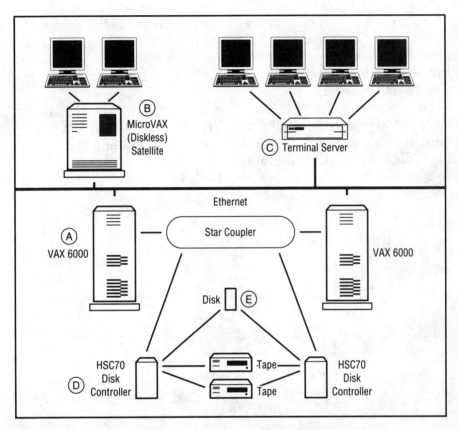

FIGURE 5.1 A VAX cluster lets two or more CPUs share storage and other peripherals. It provides high-speed access and high availability. The various CPUs in a cluster combine their power to provide enhanced computing. [Reprinted with permission of Digital Equipment Corporation.]

and the computers themselves and their data across multiple CPUs.

VAXcluster software supports three hardware configurations: Computer interconnect (CI) systems, Ethernet-based local area VAXclusters (LAVC), and mixed interconnect (LAVC Phase II).

The computer interconnect bus is a high-speed, dual path connection that links up to 24 nodes in a loosely coupled configuration. A node can be either a VAX CPU or an intelligent I/O controller called the Hierarchical Storage Controller (HSC).

The connection is made with four coaxial cables up to 135 feet long. The cables run from a CI adapter in the VAX to a Digital

Star Coupler unit. The maximum distance between processors is 270 feet—135 feet from each CPU to the star coupler. CI cluster systems primarily connect large digital processors and units in the 6000 series. Consider this the "computer room" cluster solution (see Figure 5.2).

LAVC systems are primarily for MicroVAXs, units that don't have the high-speed parallel bus. The Ethernet-based LAVC system affords some of the same cluster advantages enjoyed by the big machines for departmental work groups.

In mixed interconnect systems both Ethernet and CI connections are used. This arrangement brings high-end and smaller

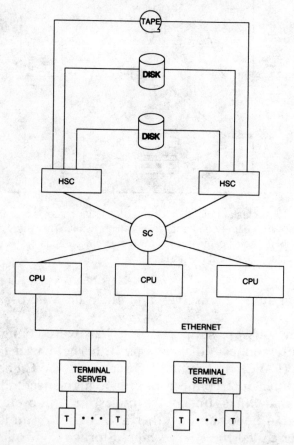

FIGURE 5.2 The basic components of a VAX cluster system include two or more CPUs, HSC controllers, disk or tape, and a star coupler. [Reprinted with permission of Digital Equipment Corporation.]

VAX systems together into a single cluster environment. The mixed interconnect configuration requires VMS 5.0 or later (see Figure 5.3).

The CI link uses one cable for transmitting and one for receiving on each path, so four cables are required for each VAX in the cluster. Data moves over a cluster connection at up to 70 Mbits per second and includes user data as well as control information.

This redundant system keeps a single failure from interrupting VAXcluster operations. In addition, no single node in the cluster operates as a master, so any node can be removed or added without keeping other nodes from working together. Traffic is transmitted on either of the two paths, depending on which one is available at any given time. When both paths are available, data moves faster than when only one path is used. VMS systems

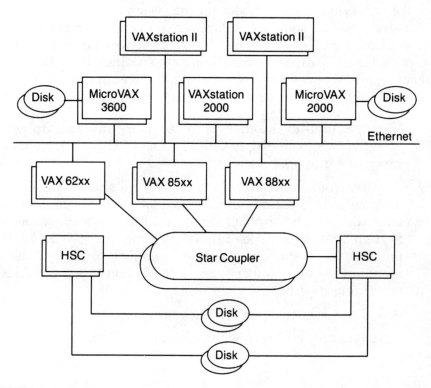

FIGURE 5.3 A Local Area VAX cluster can combine large and small hosts into an efficient, shared configuration. This LAVC Phase II configuration shows the mix of Ethernet clustering with CI-bus clusters. [Reprinted with permission of Digital Equipment Corporation.]

periodically check a failed path so that as soon as a down path comes back on line it can be used.

The star coupler sits between individual VAXs in the cluster and distributes data simultaneously to all the nodes in the VAXcluster system. The CI adapter, which mounts inside the processor and connects to the CI bus, monitors the channel to determine whether it is being addressed.

The star coupler accepts up to 24 node connections under ideal conditions. The coupler sits in the middle of a cluster, serving as the common connection point for all the nodes in the system arranged in a radial or star configuration.

This is a passive coupler that simply uses splitter/combiner transformers to exchange signals among the systems in the cluster. The dual ports of the CI bus are electrically isolated from each other, so you can add or remove a VAX node without affecting the operation of other nodes on the system.

Clustering offers some advantages over Ethernet or other connections among processors. Data transfer between nodes is seven times faster than Ethernet based on raw specifications. But the advantage may be even greater because of lower overhead on the bus. In addition, clustered systems enjoy these features:

- High availability through the redundant links and storage group access for multiple CPUs. If one CPU goes down you can still get to your data.

- Simultaneous multisystem file and record sharing. In addition, with VAX Volume Shadowing software, all data written to disk can be duplicated on multiple physical volumes. System and data disks can be volume shadowed. Each member of a shadow group is identical to every other member. If any member fails, data I/O continues with the remaining members.

- Broad range of cost/performance options.

- Easy recovery and reconfiguration after a node failure.

HSC

The HSC connects multiple hosts to a set of disks or tape. The HSC functions as a node in the cluster and communicates with the hosts over the CI bus using the Digital MSCP (Mass Storage Control Protocol). The communications from the HSC to the storage devices use the Standard Disk Interface (SDI) and Standard Tape Interface (STI) protocols. The SDI/STI interfaces are passively coupled so they can be connected or disconnected without affecting other devices in the cluster system.

The HSC maximizes throughput by handling multiple, concurrent operations on multiple drives and optimizes the physical operations, such as track seeks and rotational positioning.

Two models of the HSC are available, the HSC40 and the HSC70. The HSC40 supports up to six SDI or STI interfaces and the HSC70 supports eight. Each SDI supports up to four RA-compatible disks so that an HSC40 can connect up to 24 disks and each HSC70 can connect up to 32 disks. Also, each STI can support four master tape drives.

Digital recommends the use of terminal servers to attach terminals to a terminal system. Terminal servers are discussed in more detail later in the chapter.

The various systems in a cluster can be controlled through the VAXcluster console system, which issues console commands such as booting systems and running offline diagnostics, and examines operating messages.

Each console can control up to 24 devices, which can be nodes in a VAXcluster, standalone systems, or third-party equipment—anything that sends ASCII data over a serial line and supports XON/XOFF and I/O buffering.

LAVC

Local Area VAX Cluster configurations are slower than a CI connection because CPU-to-CPU traffic—commands and data—travel over 10 Mbps Ethernet instead of the 70 Mbps CI channel. Otherwise, however, LAVC brings clustering functionality to MicroVAX machines that lack the CI bus.

VAXcluster software supports resource sharing over the members of the cluster, including disk resources, tapes, and printers.

With an LAVC configuration all of the disks on all systems in the cluster can be accessed from any node. In addition, the processors themselves are shared resources. Users submit batch jobs to run on specific systems in the cluster. And you can store a single copy of the operating systems and applications on a central disk drive, reducing storage overhead and, through dual porting of the drives to two host systems, the data remains available to the cluster nodes even if the primary system fails.

In an LAVC system you can also have diskless members because the central storage devices can be shared.

In a Phase II LAVC system, some of the systems use Ethernet alone as the data and command link, while others use the CI bus. This arrangement lets high-end and low-end systems participate almost as peers in a cluster. Such a mixed system supports up to 42 VAX nodes as long as the total number of CI-based systems doesn't exceed 24.

Cluster systems are compared in the following list:

CI	LAVC	Phase II
Multiple large VAXs	MicroVAXs	All VAX systems
70 Mbps CI Channel	10 Mbps Ethernet	70Mbps/10Mbps
HSC Storage Controller	Local Disk I/O	Both
Star Coupler	Ethernet	Both

DSSI CLUSTERING OF 3000-SERIES MICROVAXS

With the introduction of the 3000-series of enhanced performance MicroVAXs, Digital unveiled a new dual-host bus configuration that provides VAXcluster performance without the need for BI/CI bus machines.

The Digital Storage Systems Interconnect (DSSI) bus supports the linking of two 3000-series machines that can share storage on the new DSSI bus. An integral part of the design is a new disk drive interface called ISE, for integrated storage element. This design puts much of the electronics and logic of handling the disk drive onboard the drive itself. Such a close link between the drive controller and its physical elements offers some potential advantages. Higher throughput can result from the close coupling and the fact that the host CPU is removed from at least part of its traditional drive management duties. Figure 5.4 shows DSSI clustering configurations.

Configuration Examples

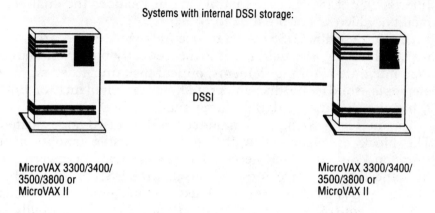

Systems with internal DSSI storage:

DSSI

MicroVAX 3300/3400/
3500/3800 or
MicroVAX II

MicroVAX 3300/3400/
3500/3800 or
MicroVAX II

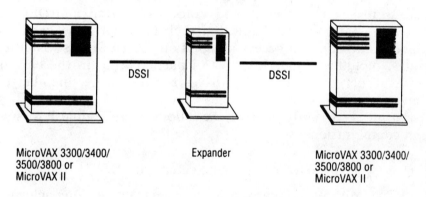

Systems with a DSSI storage pedestal:

DSSI   DSSI

MicroVAX 3300/3400/
3500/3800 or
MicroVAX II

Expander

MicroVAX 3300/3400/
3500/3800 or
MicroVAX II

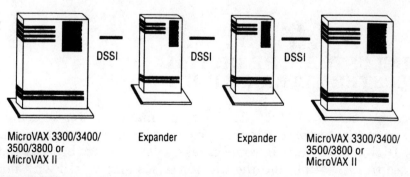

Two MicroVAX systems with no storage in the system pedestals:

DSSI   DSSI   DSSI

MicroVAX 3300/3400/
3500/3800 or
MicroVAX II

Expander

Expander

MicroVAX 3300/3400/
3500/3800 or
MicroVAX II

FIGURE 5.4   DSSI clustering takes three basic configurations, using MicroVAX 3xxx
CPUs. [Reprinted with permission of Digital Equipment Corporation.]

Technically DSSI is similar to SCSI (Small Computer System Interface), but it is not compatible and it includes the dual port facility, which is not possible in SCSI.

Digital describes DSSI as "a device independent bus architecture." The design is such that it is theoretically possible to build tape integrated storage elements, optical disk integrated storage elements, solid state disk integrated storage elements, or anything else that moves data in large quantities.

The dual host configuration under DSSI is a two-node cluster. The block management traffic and the cluster management traffic are routed over Ethernet. The storage traffic between the host and the disk drive is routed through the DSSI bus. It is theoretically possible to route the cluster management and block management traffic over the DSSI bus, and Digital reportedly is considering that strategy.

To make a 3000-series cluster work you'll need ISE drives in both units to be clustered, and VMS, VAXcluster, and DECnet software. With this configuration each MicroVAX can serve as a boot node and can access all ISEs on the DSSI bus. Satellite nodes, including other MicroVAXs participating in the cluster via Ethernet, can access ISE drives through either member of the dual host cluster.

Digital is currently offering the following three dual host system configurations:

- A two-MicroVAX cluster connected with DSSI

- Two MicroVAXs that share one storage expansion enclosure

- Two MicroVAXs that share two storage expansion enclosures

SI CLUSTOR: THE DIGITAL CLUSTER ALTERNATIVE

System Industries, Inc. is a storage manufacturer offering a series of Clustor products that provide cluster-type performance for Digital hardware. In some cases the features are broader than those from Digital, and the Clustor series also works with non-BI bus machines.

SI has developed its own series of host interface cards that, it says, offer high-performance data transfers without loading down the bus. Interfaces for BI, SBI, Unibus, CMI, Cache, and Q-bus are available.

One reason for the SI development, according to company officials, was to allow people more full use of MicroVAXs. The company believes the popular 3000-series MicroVAXs are attractive because of high performance and relatively low price. However, they are limited because they lack a BI channel and can be clustered only through the local area VAX cluster.

SI views a shared computer environment from a different perspective than Digital. Processors attached to Clustor drives are considered peripherals to the storage device instead of the other way around. With Clustor, you can treat a MicroVAX just like a VAX 8800, as a processor that is peripheral to a central storage.

Clustor systems consist of a 68010-based controller that can support up to 16 high-capacity hard drives and eight VAX CPUs, and a bus interface for the host machine.

Clustor consists of two configurations, the Clustor 3 and the Clustor 5. The Clustor 3 offers a minimum of two drives in a 60-inch cabinet with SILINK cluster software, the disk controller, and a single computer port adapter (CPA). The Clustor 5 adds another 68000-family microprocessor for cache management, eight megabytes of cache memory, and a performance display unit (PDU).

The company's CPAs are an important part of the performance advantage claimed for the Clustor product, according to the company. SI calls the Q-bus a high performance bus, but adds that "unfortunately there just isn't a well-designed Q-bus interface from Digital that makes use of that full Q-bus bandwidth."

SI adapters permit location of host CPUs up to 150 feet from the Clustor controller, officials say, and the system permits each host to maintain its own local storage in addition to the shared Clustor disks. The Clustor controller supports most older disk drives, permitting customers to upgrade existing systems. In addition, it is compatible with new and future drives.

Clustor is promoted as a true multitasking controller. As additional hosts are added, relative Clustor performance is improved because you can overlap a lot of system overhead. It does true overlap seeks, conducting a seek on one drive while it is doing DMA (direct memory access) on another drive.

The PDU is a front panel LED (light emitting diode) display that shows six key performance characteristics in both numeric averages and instantaneous, moving bar displays. The performance characteristics monitored are cache hit rate, average drive access time, number of input/output requests per second, the write load (read-to-write ratio), the data transfer size, and the average seek distance.

SI pioneered this form of performance display, according to company president Bob Duncan. Older 9900 series SI drives can use an optional, separate PDU panel. The new design integrates the performance measurement displays with the main controller panel.

The display is considered a management tool, and the company defends it as "not just a bunch of pretty lights." A conscientious system manager who watches this information can get an indication of when the disk is becoming fragmented, then manually position data and watch the results with the bar graphs, SI claims.

During one brief demonstration we witnessed of a PDU display operating in conjunction with SI's own corporate CPU, disk cache access was running an average of 77 percent of total data requests with periods as high as 100 percent. Officials say averages of up to a 90 percent performance improvement are possible in I/O intensive environments.

Access time is a component of seek and latency on the drive. If you are using a high performance drive with 15 to 16 milliseconds (ms) seek time, the Clustor controller and cache can give you access to frequently used data in one to five ms as compared to 20 ms. That is an aspect of throughput that is a by-product of the drive working with the controller and the 8MB of cache, SI officials said.

SI is targeting the Clustor device toward existing customers who are using older 9900 controllers in a cluster system with 700- and 8600-family CPUs, and to users who want to cluster MicroVAXs with multiple 8000-family systems.

By combining Clustor with Digital LAVC software you should be able to get MicroVAX cluster performance close to full HSC/-CI/BI systems from Digital.

SI's Clustor system provides VAXcluster performance in the MicroVAX environment, the company claims, by taking all data transfer off of Ethernet and putting it on a direct bus-level channel. Multiple Clustor controllers can be connected to increase the number of supported drives and CPUs or to provide fault-tolerant redundancy. The Clustor controller groups physical drives into logical units so that no more than eight physical drives are presented to any CPU at a given time. An optional control panel allows users to configure specific Clustor drives for exclusive use by individual CPUs.

DECNET

DECnet is the most common of Vax-to-Vax links. It can be used to carry VAX cluster commands and data, as described in the SI discussion. It also carries the long-distance leg of terminal server, gateway and bridge links, and it ties together VAX CPUs within a room, a building, a campus, or around the world.

Normally VAX systems connect over DECnet using one of the three common Ethernet media: Thick wire, thin wire, or twisted pair. These direct-connect attachments only work when the hardware to be linked is in relatively close proximity. Otherwise DECnet must be extended through special facilities. A large company such as Digital has these special communications facilities, and third-party solutions also are available.

DECROUTER 2000

The Digital DECrouter 2000 shown in Figure 5.5 is a combination hardware/software product that routes information between DECnet LANs running over Ethernet. One port of the router attaches to the Ethernet and up to four additional ports can be used for synchronous communications to other LANs at up to 64K bps, or if only two lines are used, at speeds up to 256K bps.

Use the DECrouter 2000 when you have remote LANs running DECnet and you want continuous communication among the nodes on the two networks, in which case you need two DECrouter 2000s, one for each network.

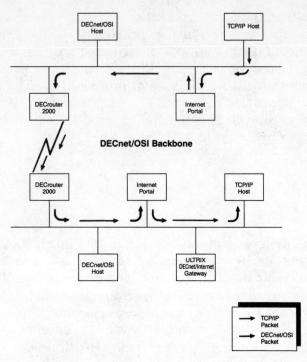

FIGURE 5.5 The DECrouter 2000 can provide wide area network connectivity for DECnet/OSI and TCP/IP hosts. [Reprinted with permission of Digital Equipment Corporation.]

Additionally, this router can be used for remote node attachment to a single Ethernet LAN through remote dial-up or dedicated serial lines (though the slower DECrouter 200 probably is a better choice if you only have modem links).

X25 ROUTER 2000

The Digital X25 Router 2000 serves as a packet switched gateway for Ethernet networks (See Figure 5.6). Coupled with the Packet System Interface (PSI) software access, this package gives users on an Ethernet LAN easy access to the X.25 network. It supports DECnet and X.25 protocols on the same router.

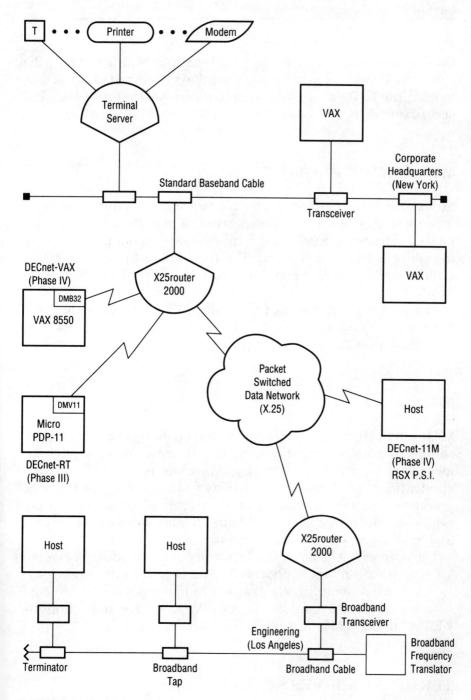

FIGURE 5.6   The X25 Router 2000 can connect remote Digital and Non-Digital nodes through an X.25 network. In addition, this router performs conventional routing functions of the DECrouter 2000. [Reprinted with permission of Digital Equipment Corporation.]

One benefit of this box is the interface it provides through the packet switched network to multivendor systems. It offers access to multiple PSDNs for any system on the LAN that runs VAX PSI access software.

METROWAVE BRIDGE

Suppose you want to extend Ethernet across natural or man-made barriers. With this microwave-based system you can link LANs that are as much as 4.5 miles apart, as long as they are in line-of-sight of each other. The metrowave bridge can be an economical solution when it is difficult or impossible to pull cables between sites.

In addition to supporting full 10 Mbps Ethernet links, the same microwave system can carry other T1 transmissions, such as voice and video.

MAILBUS

MAILbus is Digital's X.400 application enabling users and applications to exchange mail or messages in a multivendor environment (see Figure 5.7). Basically, MAILbus is a set of software applications that link email systems from a variety of vendors' products. The system can tie mail systems together in a corporate-wide electronic mail backbone. It also supports electronic mail exchange with public electronic mail systems.

The core of MAILbus is the Message Router module, a layered VMS application that supports store and forward messaging service, as well as enabling the transfer of messages across the mail network. MAILbus can run on any VAX system that supports DECnet under VMS Version 5.0 or later.

TERMINAL SERVERS

Serial transmission is extremely important within a department or company building, for dial-up links and for certain dir-

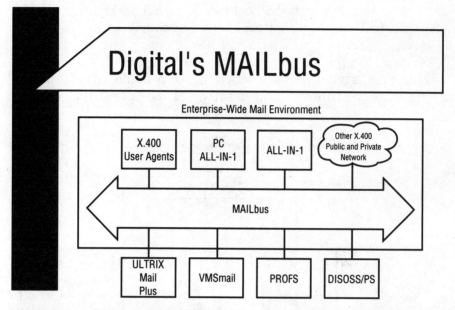

Digital's MAILbus

Enterprise-Wide Mail Environment

X.400 User Agents — PC ALL-IN-1 — ALL-IN-1 — Other X.400 Public and Private Network

MAILbus

ULTRIX Mail Plus — VMSmail — PROFS — DISOSS/PS

FIGURE 5.7 Digital's MAILBus provides X.400 connectivity for standards-based links throughout an enterprise. [Reprinted with permission of Digital Equipment Corporation.]

ect connections. (See Chapter 6 for more information on serial links.)

You can connect terminals and desktop computers directly to a VAX through an appropriate communications controller that plugs directly into the VAX, or you can use a serial terminal server. A terminal server accepts a few or even hundreds of serial devices, buffers the inputs, and sends the data over DECnet to any of the computers active on the line.

The original terminal servers, while still sophisticated devices, conducted fairly basic operations. Current terminal servers are more complicated, of necessity, to operate in a computing environment that includes hardware from multiple vendors, a mix of minicomputers, workstations, PCs, and terminals, and heavily distributed applications.

In a Digital-only world with local terminals, a terminal server setup can still be fairly simple. You need one or more boxes with enough serial lines to accommodate your terminals and a DECnet connection to reach the host (see Figure 5.8). You'll probably choose a LAT-compatible (local area transport) solution.

However, today's VAX manager also has to contend with non-VAX hosts, foreign peripherals, workstations, and PCs. Moreover, any current system configuration must provide the flexibility to grow in the future as the number of users and the amount

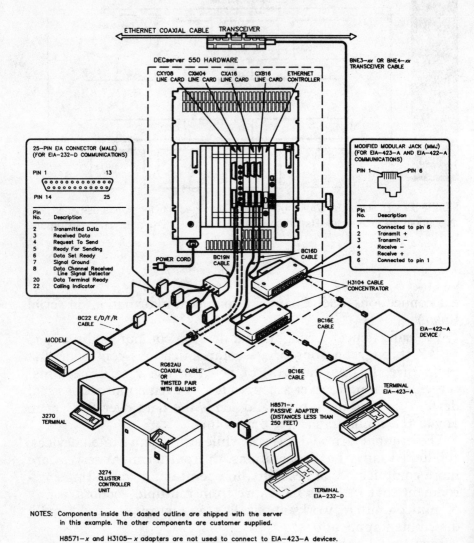

FIGURE 5.8 Digital's high-end terminal server, the 550, is a VAX-based platform that can work with a variety of serial devices. [Reprinted with permission of Digital Equipment Corporation.]

of networked hardware increases. In this situation, selecting a terminal server may not be a simple process.

For one thing, a LAT-only solution in a multivendor shop may not get everybody connected. UNIX hosts and workstations, for example, are probably using TCP/IP. VAX users connected through a LAT terminal can't talk to these CPUs, and the TCP users can't get to the VAX.

Although Digital does not have a LAT-TCP/IP solution in a single box yet, they are working on such a device. The majority of third-party vendors do have terminal servers that support both protocols, however.

In addition to choosing terminal servers that support the protocols that are used on the network to which they are attached, users may also need to consider which physical network connections are supported. Most of the available terminal server products support both thick and thin wire Ethernet in the same box (see Figure 5.9). In addition, products such as Datability's

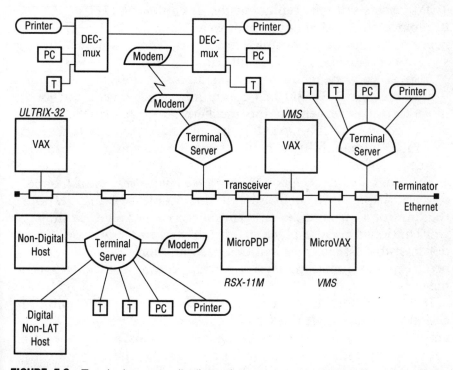

FIGURE 5.9 Terminal servers distribute the serial connections, simplifying wiring schemes. [Reprinted with permission of Digital Equipment Corporation.]

Vista—also available through Dilog—offer twisted pair Ethernet support.

Although TCP/IP is not yet used widely in the Digital environment, many vendors predict that the ability to have both LAT and TPC/IP capabilities in the same terminal server will become important, probably before the end of 1990.

In fact, officials at Datability's hardware division tell us that buyers are concerned about TCP/IP even if they don't have immediate applications, and many are asking for dual capability as a hedge against future needs.

Among the questions purchasers need to answer when configuring a LAT/TCP system is whether TCP users on a network can access a LAT host, and vice versa. Whether or not this cross-protocol support is automatic is another consideration.

In addition, if an existing network already is heavily committed to one protocol or the other, it may be important for a new server product to be able to use equipment already installed. Can users attached through a DECserver 200, for example, access TCP/IP hosts without replacing the Digital server? If you have to replace all existing equipment to achieve the TCP or LAT connection, additional cost and effort must be considered during system configuration and justification.

Also, if you are using newer terminals it may be important to be able to use 38,400 bps communications speeds. Although most terminal servers in the marketplace support 38.4 Kbps, a few do not. If this speed is important in your application, consider the capabilities of the terminal server hardware you are configuring.

Terminal server buyers also are faced with issues of technology and expansibility. In all but the simplest of installations, the days of a straight serial terminal server may be waning. As workstations take the place of "dumb" terminals and multivendor host-to-host communications become more important, users need broader functionality from their communications equipment.

In fact, some vendors are calling their products "communications servers" instead of terminal servers. Datability, for example, believes in positioning communications facilities on the network instead of within a host machine, thereby allowing terminals, workstations, or hosts access to communications facilities as necessary. The Vista product is one of a class of bus-based communications products that can be expanded with the addition of one or more additional cards. Users can add 8- or 32-port communications cards to the Vista bus, for example, or substitute a multiport modem for one of the serial cards.

The Protocol Gateway card is one of the latest additions to the Vista line. A single protocol card can handle up to 16 simultaneous logical sessions, converting between any two onboard network protocols. This capability allows TCP/IP users to access LAT hosts and vice versa without replacing existing hardware because each user is provided with the proper prompts and protocols to support transparent cross-protocol communications.

Digital has recognized the need for both Digital and TCP/IP protocols with the announcement of the DECnet/Internet Router 2000, a combination of an Internet portal with the existing DECrouter 2000. The package provides TCP/IP and DECnet connectivity at up to 2 Mbps/s. The Internet Portal is based on Digital's RISC-based DECsystem 3100 hardware.

Digital's conventional terminal servers offer LAT, of course, but they don't support TCP/IP. However, the company recognizes the importance of the TCP protocol and promises to provide short- and long-term solutions as the industry moves toward full OSI compliance.

Although TCP/IP is not a controlled standard, it is a wide-reaching one. However, it may not adequately support very large users with international connections, and OSI standards will most likely replace TCP/IP for these applications.

For local connections of terminals to hosts, however, LAT still is the most efficient protocol. It is an important protocol because Digital reports that 80 to 90 percent of terminal users who want access to a host want to connect to a local host.

Digital's advice to potential terminal server purchasers is to learn all they can about their network configuration. A centralized network where all host machines are in one place requires different solutions than those for a highly distributed network. Additionally, users are advised to fully understand their actual requirements for terminal server functionality.

The rise of competition in the terminal server market is good for the consumer, but it can also lead to confusion about what features and issues are important.

What is the major issue of the future? Desktop computing, according to Digital.

Digital figures suggest that although PCs and other workstations are moving more and more into mainstream VAX computing—and many of them attach directly to DECnet over Ethernet—the majority of these machines attach to VAX hosts using terminal emulation.

As we move into the 1990s, however, this trend is likely to change. Software that allows PCs to emulate X terminals is becoming more widely available, and relatively inexpensive terminals that function as X Window System servers attached directly to Ethernet are becoming popular. Will X terminals replace PCs on the majority of VAX environment desktops, or will they replace terminals while PCs move against full-blown workstations?

As this transition occurs, the communication server versus terminal server issue becomes even more important. So look for future products to provide more functionality and better flexibility from a broader vendor base. Even with the advent of networking standards, the terminal server question seems destined to become more—not less—complicated.

CHAPTER SUMMARY

There is no one, simple solution to connecting VAXs across an enterprise. In any given situation you will probably use a variety of connection schemes. For the highest speed, high availability, and maximum flexibility among local VAXs, the Digital VAX-cluster is the logical choice, or you could choose a third-party clustering package from a company like System Industries.

Even if you are using clustering, you will probably choose DECnet over Ethernet or twisted pair. This will let you scatter serial terminals, printers, and other peripherals at about any distance from the main CPU through the use of network attached terminal servers.

Then there is the question of serial links. You will use these for dial-up communications, for some dedicated lines, and occasionally for local file transfers.

Further, you will sometimes use a combination of these basic facilities for special case communications such as satellite, packet switched, or other links.

In the next chapter we offer some additional details on using serial links in the VAX environment.

CHAPTER **6**

Serial
Communications

Among the most basic concepts of computing is connecting devices with serial lines. VAX users frequently use a serial link from a terminal to an area terminal server or connect directly to the host. PC users in a VAX world use serial links to a modem or in conjunction with terminal emulator software to allow the PC access to the host. In the VAX world, serial printers and plotters can be distributed with terminal servers or printer servers to put the output devices where they are used, instead of clustering them around a central CPU.

Whatever the application, serial links are an important part of VAX access. In this chapter we will introduce the concepts of serial communications and define terms to help you understand the links you are using daily, and to assist you in configuring or troubleshooting them.

Most computer users probably agree that serial communications is the most difficult part of using the machines. Standards exist for connecting one computer to another, of course, but the specifications are broad enough to allow for custom features. While this may be desirable and useful for individual products, it can also make the process of connecting one computer to another more difficult.

DIAL-UP COMMUNICATIONS

Dial up computer-to-computer communications are extremely common with microcomputer users. It is easy for a desktop user to load a user-friendly software package and, with a couple of keystrokes, automatically dial a remote host, logon to the system, check for mail or other messages, copy selected data to the local hard disk, and logoff. By writing scripts—simple programs—that emulate keystroke commands, all this and more can be conducted "hands off."

An interactive session with a remote host through a desktop machine is almost as easy. Once the local software is loaded and the logon process is complete, the desktop machine behaves, in most ways, precisely like the native terminal it emulates.

Many VAX users currently enjoy similar functionality by dialing up a remote VAX from the local host (see Figure 6.1). In this

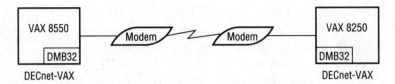

FIGURE 6.1 Basic VAX-to-VAX configuration with dial-up links using modems. [Reprinted with permission of Digital Equipment Corporation.]

case the user accesses a host-based communications program from a desktop terminal (or PC emulating a terminal), and the remote number is dialed.

Dial-up VAX-to-VAX connections provide local users with access to other company computers, to public mail services such as MCI, and to information databases such as the Ziff Davis computer library or one of the hundreds of offerings from Dialog.

The following section provides some background information on the telecommunications process.

SERIAL HARDWARE

Computers are limited in their understanding of data. While you may read As and Bs and Cs on your screen, the computer is simply taking a voltage reading to distinguish between on and off. It moves pulses of high or low voltage around the system and in and out of storage places and then takes a voltage reading to find out what kind of information is stored there.

The power of the computer comes from its ability to work with predefined "machine logic" that allows those on or off states to represent almost any kind of data or instructions. These on and off states can be stored in the machine's internal random access memory (RAM), on disk or tape, or etched into read-only silicon. When you communicate information from one machine to another, you move voltage states that represent data along a wire in some form that is interpreted by the remote machine. This native computer counting system is based on binary arithmetic, dealing solely in 0s and 1s.

All data on the computer's I/O (input/output) interface are in binary form. A "1" data bit is called a mark, and is the normal condition of the line when there is no data. The mark condition is set by a negative voltage of −3 to −25 volts. A "0" data bit is called a space, and is represented by a positive voltage of +3.

Therefore, when the computer detects an incoming signal changing from a negative voltage to a positive voltage—from a mark to a space—it determines that a 0 data bit has arrived. Various combinations of 1s and 0s represent real information: the letters of the alphabet, punctuation, and numbers. In serial communications this information is transmitted and translated one bit at a time, one after the other.

You can make the serial connection in the following two ways:

Direct connection. The output port of one machine is connected to an input port of another. Direct connect communication is fast and relatively simple, but it requires point-to-point links between machines located relatively close to each other.

Intermediate connection. Dedicated lines, dial-up links, or a combination of the two connect machines through an intermediary wired network such as a telephone system, a public telecommunications network, or a special-purpose local area network.

The task of moving those 0s and 1s from point to point is the heart of telecommunications, and it is an assignment that does not proceed in a very straightforward manner.

First, the digital signals within a computer travel in parallel—a multilane highway moving bits (1s and 0s) as computer "words" 8, 16, 32, or 64 bits wide.

The parallel bus is sometimes extended outside of the computer to form an easy link to a printer, plotter, or another computer. It is not a big deal to bring eight to sixty-four wires a few feet from the computer to another machine. However, to send the same information over longer distances, particularly over a telephone cable, you usually have only two wires.

Therefore, for most long-distance communication, the parallel output of the computer bus is converted to a serial signal in which each bit of the computer word follows after the one before it down a single data wire (the second wire is used as the return circuit from the receiver).

THE TELEPHONE NETWORK

With today's technology, any person, located almost anywhere, can communicate directly with almost anyone else in a matter of seconds. The enabling technology is the telephone network, and few residents of the developed world are ever more than a few minutes away from one of the nodes of its system. There are more than 500 million phones installed around the world.

In theory, this network of overhead wires, underground and undersea cables, microwave links, and satellite transmitters and receivers could be used for interconnection of at least 500 million computers, too. There are, though, a few difficulties arising from the generally low quality of voice grade connections.

The typical phone line has from two to four wires. Only two of the wires are used to carry data and perform all other telephone functions, including ringing the bell. A voice telephone line is technically limited to 9,600 bits per second (bps) using most standard modulation schemes, although 2400 bps is a more realistic speed. In many places, voice phone lines will not support rates that high, and are best used at 1,200 or 300 bps.

The connection from the user's office or home to the local phone company is called the local loop. If you were to call from your house to the neighbor's house across the street, the call would travel to the central office and back along this line. At the central office, there are two primary outbound links: an interoffice trunk line that connects other local central offices to each other, and a toll trunk that connects a central office to a toll office for the use of intertoll trunk lines for long-distance calls. The phone company must install amplifiers and switching devices at each office.

If you need to connect computers that are fairly close together, you can use a straight wire for the link. Beyond 50 to 1,000 feet, depending on the technology used, you have to use something else, and the telephone system is an obvious solution. However, with most voice grade systems you can't directly transmit digital signals.

The actual telephone signal is called an "analog" message—an analogy of the real sound in which louder is higher, for example. If you were to examine a graph or an oscilloscope pattern of a moment of human speech, you would see that the variations in frequency (what we call pitch) are comparable to the variations in the frequency of an electrical analog conversion of that same moment of human speech.

The typical human voice has a maximum range from deepest bass of 25 Hz to shrillest soprano of 20,000 Hz (a measurement of cycles per second pronounced hertz, and named after physicist Heinrich Hertz). Most ordinary speaking sounds fall in the range from 30 to about 3000 Hz. Because the original designers of the telephone system thought this limited range of conversational frequencies was all they would ever need, they set a bandwidth of 2300 Hz, from 700 Hz to 3000 Hz. The smaller bandwidth makes it possible to squeeze more than one two-way conversation on a single wire, with different channels at different frequencies.

PHONE LINE FACTS

Telephone signals can also be multiplexed so that individual signals are chopped up and mixed with other signals. Such schemes are in widespread use and they require precise timing and high signal quality to allow the incoming signal to be reconstructed at the receiving end.

Any phone signal suffers from attenuation—a loss of power measured in decibels—when sent over distance. This loss of strength is caused by impedance—a combination of electrical resistance from wires, switches, and connections—and by capacitive and inductive reactance. Reactance is electrical resistance that varies by frequency. As frequency increases, inductive reactance increases; capacitive reactance decreases as frequency increases.

Echo suppressors can also interfere with data. Echo is the feedback that is caused by the delay in reception between two points. To help eliminate echo, phone lines use devices called echo suppressors. Some modems can send a special signal to disable echo suppressors.

This combination of factors—limited bandwidth, data division through multiplexing, interference and distortion caused by switches, and the general assortment of noise and interference that distorts most voice grade calls—explain why data communications over telephone lines can be difficult.

PRIVATE SOLUTIONS

For some applications it may be economical to bypass the telephone company in favor of using your own lines when locations are relatively close together. For longer distances you can contract with the telephone company and other third parties to supply and maintain alternate communications links for you.

LEASED LINES

One choice open to heavy users of telecommunications circuits is a private or leased line.

The basic voice line is a switched line with no fixed link between any two telephone instruments. In fact, on a long-distance call from New York to Miami, for example, it is quite possible for the link to be switched through Dallas or Chicago at some times.

A leased line, on the other hand, is a direct link from point A to point B. You are guaranteed ready access and provided some protection against loss of quality from path switching. Such a dedicated line is relatively expensive, but if you are spending a lot of time on dial-up links over the public telephone system anyway, you can probably justify the cost through savings on long-distance charges, faster data transfer, and better overall line quality.

The most expensive telephone option is something called a conditioned line. This is a special dedicated line with additional telephone company equipment and circuitry promising higher quality circuits, which may include an increased bandwidth.

Economic analysis should be considered in deciding which type of line best meets your needs. If you will need to connect two points once or twice a day for transmission of a relatively short duration, a standard dial-up (switched) telephone circuit at each end is probably your best bet. A dial-up line also allows the user to connect with other gateways. On the other hand, if two offices in the same city need to be in constant communication for transmission of critical information, a leased line may be the best alternative, and in certain circumstances less expensive than paying time charges on a dial-up line.

INDEPENDENT COMMON CARRIERS

Another major alternative is to use one of the value added networks, also called public data networks. Companies such as Tymnet (owned by McDonnell Douglas) and Telenet (from GTE), for example, may serve your long-distance data communications needs. These networks typically have entrance points in most major metropolitan areas that can be contacted with a local call. These points, called concentrators, add incoming data from local users to the heavy traffic of packets of information on the nationwide circuits.

These competitors to AT&T plug into the system at the toll office level. (If you have problems with your local telephone service, you're not going to get much satisfaction from an alternate carrier until you come up with a direct link to them that does not use the local loop.)

If your company is large enough, you might consider employing the services of a telecommunications consultant to examine all of your options, including the possible purchase and installation of PBX (Private Branch Exchange) systems, WATS (Wide Area Telephone Service) lines for incoming and outgoing calls, and other special services.

CONVERTING DATA FOR COMMUNICATIONS

We have shown how information inside the computer is stored as varying voltage levels (digital information), and how this data can be moved in parallel or serial form. To transceive this data through a communications link such as a telephone system, however, the information must be converted into a form compatible with the link used.

A modem (a contraction of MOdulator/DEModulator) is one device that makes that conversion. A modem modulates an incoming digital signal into an analog waveform for transmission, and performs the opposite function as a receiver, demodulating the analog signal back into digital pulses.

THE MODEM

A modem translates the 0s and 1s of the digital signal into one of four distinct frequencies within the telephone line's narrow bandwidth. A modem identified as an originating device uses one end of the band, with a modem operating in the answer mode using the other end.

The mechanism for movement of the high-low warble of a stream of bits is called a carrier signal. This is a continuous audible tone exchanged between a pair of modems. Technically, the modem carrier signal is a fixed frequency sine wave—a signal of one strength or amplitude. The waves cycle from positive to negative and back again, and the more cycles per unit of time the higher the pitch of the tone. This tone is altered, or modulated, by the modem to represent the 0s and 1s of the signal.

The carrier tone itself can be modulated in a number of ways including:

Amplitude modulation. The height of the wave, representing the strength or voltage level of the signal, is altered.

Frequency modulation. The number of cycles per second (measured in Hertz) is varied to represent information.

Phase angle modulation. Information is conveyed by the angle, relative to the previous cycle, at which the cycle crosses the 0 axis.

Most often used is a form of frequency modulation referred to as FSK, and a form of phase angle modulation called PSK.

FSK stands for frequency shift keying. This system uses two different frequencies to represent 0 and 1. The originate device has one pair of frequencies, while the answer device has another.

PSK is the abbreviation for phase shift keying. Picture a continuous horizontal line as representing the 0 point. Rising from the 0 point in a smooth curve is a sine wave. At its peak above the 0 line, the signal represents a +1; dropping back down in a smooth curve, it represents 0 when it crosses the base line. Continuing in a curve below the baseline, it represents −1 at its lowest point; arcing back up to the baseline, it registers a 0 once more. Therefore, an unmodulated sine wave passes from 0 to +1 to 0 to −1 and back to 0 in one complete phase, or 360 degrees. PSK changes or modulates the sine wave so that the angle at which it crosses the baseline represents information, specifically the 1s or 0s of binary communication.

The PSK standard used in modems goes one step further, having the changes in phase representing two bits at a time, in a character called a dibit. The dibit can be 00, 01, 10, or 11. From any one point of a phase, an alteration can be plus or minus 90 degrees, plus 180 degrees, or no change.

TRANSMISSION SPEEDS

Data inside a computer moves at tens of thousands of bits per second or even faster. But serial communications speeds are much, much slower since the bits that comprise each computer word must line up one behind the other before they can be sent down the line.

Another major limiting factor on transmission speed is the physical capacity of a telecommunications channel, principally its bandwidth. You could think of bandwidth as the diameter of the pipe—obviously, the larger the pipe, the more information or the more channels of information can be carried at one instant. In electrical terms, bandwidth is the difference between the highest and lowest frequencies that can flow through a channel.

By limiting the bandwidth of voice quality lines, phone companies can cram extra lines onto the same cable. It makes little difference to the quality of voice communication, but it does limit the speed of data transmission.

THE BAUD RATE

The speed of transmission of communications data is called the baud rate, which is defined as the number of discrete signal changes per time unit. The term baud is derived from the name of Emile Baudot, early pioneer in telecommunications, and it was originally a measure of dots and dashes on telegraph lines.

For 300 baud and slower standard communication, each discrete signal change using FSK modulation represents a single on or off bit, and therefore the baud rate is equivalent to the number of bits per second. At 300 baud, using computer words with eight bits to a character plus one start bit and two stop bits, the modem is transmitting an average of about 27 ASCII characters per second—about 5 words a second or 300 words a minute.

Comparison of baud rate and information throughput with high-speed modems is more complex because most such devices transmit dibits, tribits or quadbits–signals that represent more than one bit. A so-called 1,200 baud modem is in most cases actually a 600 baud device—it transmits 600 dibits, each representing two characters, per second. This equates to four times the throughput of a 300 baud device, and manufacturers have adopted the shorthand of calling their units 1,200 baud modems. The most precise way to describe these modems is as 1,200 bit per second devices.

A less precise way of looking at baud rate is to equate it with words per minute. Based on a computer word length plus framing bits totaling 11 bits per character, and based on an average English language word length of 5.5 characters, a 300 baud modem can transmit about 300 words per minute; a 1,200 baud unit about 1,200 words per minute, and so on. Obviously, this equation does not work for transmission of numbers or programming, and it may not work for transmission of technical or foreign languages that have a different average word length.

Although telecommunications is an important and necessary part of getting full use from a computer system, it can be a complicated process. By understanding some of the basics of telephone system operation, binary data storage, serial and parallel communications, and how a modem functions, you can make the process more manageable.

There are an almost unlimited number of options available in establishing the rules for telecommunications. We can choose the number of bits that make up a word (typically 7 or 8, but occasionally 5 or 6); we can decide to include parity checking or other error-checking or correction schemes (and select from one of dozens of different algorithms); we can determine the "framing" of computer words—how the computer is told where one word ends and the next begins—from one of several start/stop schemes; and we can choose the transmission speed.

The communications port is usually responsible for establishing the various protocols, but these selections must also be supported by the modem. Choosing 2,400 baud communication on the adapter will not make a 300-baud modem work any faster, for example.

The speed of telephone line communications is increasing. Whereas a few years ago a 1,200 baud modem was considered a high speed device, today almost no new modems are being sold that are slower than 2,400 baud. With better electronics and improved software routines 4,800, 9,600, and even 19,200 baud modems are possible. Note, however, that with conventional dial-up lines the actual throughput on these high-speed modems may be slower than its rating.

However, with data compression routines that remove repetitive data on one end before the transmission begins and put it back in on the other side, true 9,600 baud and faster transmissions on telephone lines are possible.

Digital and third-party vendors offer a wide variety of communications controllers to attach VAXs to other VAXs, PDP-series computers, workstations, and terminals. A controller such as the synchronous DSV11, for example, can support DECnet operations at up to 256 Kbps (bits per second) for a single line or 64 Kbps for two-line connections.

For lower-speed connections, the DZQ11 series and similar products support 9600 bps connections. Such devices are used to communicate between Q-bus computers—the MicroVAX line—and the PDP-11 series, for example.

CHAPTER SUMMARY

Serial communication, while a ubiquitous technology, is not always easily understood or applied. Terminals, PCs, printers, plotters, modems, and other devices use serial links frequently in the VAX marketplace.

The key to success is understanding the basics and learning how to work with the idiosyncrasies of individual products. If you use computers, you will inevitably be involved with serial communication. Use this chapter as a reference point to help you with the basics.

In the next chapter we provide a network checklist to help you evaluate your communications requirements, including some guidelines on planning and pricing.

Network
Checklist

Too many computer installations lack planning. Initially, needs are small and they can be handled with relatively simple solutions. As applications grow and more users become involved, the complex process of adding hardware and software has to be considered. Proper planning is important in any computer facility, but when intercommunications—networking—is involved, the planning step is even more critical.

Even if networking isn't part of the initial hardware installation, you should plan for it in the future. Without doubt, any user of Digital Equipment Corporation VAXs will eventually want to interconnect multiple VAXs or PCs and workstations with a VAX host.

A NETWORKING AUDIT

Part of your computer facility planning should be a detailed analysis of present and projected needs. Estimates of both acquisition costs and operating expenses once the network is installed should be included. Note that studies have shown that only about one-third of the total five-year cost of installing and maintaining a network are attributed to acquisition; the rest is consumed by operating expenses. (The Index Group, Inc., 1989)

Careful consideration of your perceived and projected networking needs is important. It means providing realistic and accurate estimates to avoid the problems of overplanning or underplanning your configuration.

Especially in the VAX world (as opposed to PC-only installations) where equipment costs generally go beyond a single department's ability to make purchase decisions, it is easy to get caught up in overinvolvement of various interest groups within a company.

Input from all potential users is important for determining usage needs and the physical requirements of connecting disparate user groups. However, this type of investigation should be conducted by a committee or study group that has enough authority to make initial purchase and configuration decisions.

If you appoint a study committee but do not give the group enough authority to make progress beyond gathering data, the configuration and purchase process will be short-circuited.

In addition, a reasonable time frame for the investigation and configuration planning should be established. Committees representing a variety of interest groups can get caught up in addressing every last need and concern, causing them to get sidetracked from the final goal by scheduling "just one more meeting" to work out differences.

If everyone involved understands that the planning process has a definite end point and that the time frame will not be extended except for extremely unusual circumstances, the initial planning process can move more directly toward the final goal.

In large companies this planning committee could be relatively large, with representatives from each of the major company divisions. In this case a chairman and a small subcommittee of three to five members should be appointed to direct the activities of the larger group. By conducting preliminary planning sessions and presenting suggestions to each meeting of the full committee, this subcommittee can eliminate a lot of unproductive discussion that naturally occurs when a very large group thrashes out decisions.

Department heads or division leaders can further streamline the process by providing the committee with some initial direction, including guidelines on time frame, budget considerations, and intra-company goals. In addition, group managers should be informed of the activities of committee members as work progresses and they should be willing to allow for the time and energy required from dedicated members of such a study committee.

For the company to pull together toward the common goal of improving intra-company communications through networking, a high degree of cooperation at all levels is required. Workers who are involved in committee work won't have as much time to devote to their regular jobs. We have seen network planning grind to a halt after a few weeks simply because no one made allowances for the extra work, expecting full output from employees on their regular jobs while demanding considerable time and creative energy be devoted to the planning duties.

Even if you have to hire temporary personnel to assume responsibility for some ongoing duties of personnel involved in network planning, the end result will be worth it. You will avoid alienating staff by requiring them to do extra work, and the ultimate goal of formulating a networking strategy can be reached easier.

In addition to hardware and labor costs of network installation you must be prepared to absorb expenses incurred during this planning stage. Even if you don't hire full-time or temporary people during the process, the employees you have will be sidetracked from their regular duties until the planning and installation are complete.

As an initial working document, the appropriate personnel should ask—and answer in detail—some or all of the following questions and others that are specific for your company or applications.

What computer resources already exist in the company? Which of these resources should be connected during the initial network installation? Undoubtedly, you'll consider connecting all of the VAXs on the network, but what about the Macintosh microcomputers, IBM-compatible PCs, Sun workstations, and other devices. While you are planning a network, don't neglect the less obvious users. While initial needs may not dictate that everyone in an enterprise be connected, the more capability you have for intercommunications, the more users will want and need it.

What functions or capabilities will be offered over the network: file sharing, file transfer, printer sharing, distributed software applications, and shared storage? Make a list of resources already in place that might logically be shared.

How many functions from list #2 can be accommodated with the available resources identified in list #1? What additional hardware and software will be required to accomplish your goals of function and capability? Review both lists and make sure you have added enough margin for growth in terms of both facilities and applications. Remember, it is easier to plan—within reason—for the future before much actual work is completed.

Where are resources located? What physical facilities will be required to connect them? Draw a rough map of your organization including various departments, offices, sections, and equipment. Can you identify logical work groups that might be served by their own LAN driven by a departmental VAX or PC network?

What are the potential problems in connecting these various groups? Consider building construction (are there concrete walls and floors to be traversed, for example), distances between groups and facilities, compatibility of computer systems to be bridged, and sources of potential electromagnetic interference. Draw a schematic of facilities, including existing wiring, conduits, air conditioners, wiring closets, and the like.

Can existing wiring, conduits, and other facilities be used in your planned network? For local work group computing, existing telephone wiring in new buildings can frequently be used for twisted pair Ethernet, for example. If your building is relatively new, there may be coaxial cable already in the walls, installed as part of the initial design or left from a previous installation.

Existing facilities can be useful if what they are and where they go are clearly identifiable. Consult the building owner or architect for wiring diagrams and facilities lists to make the process easier. Appoint one or two people to conduct a quick audit of the physical facilities, and include inspecting crawl ways, wiring closets, and under floor plenums in the inventory. If existing wiring is diagramed and/or carefully numbered and labeled, you should consider using it. On the other hand, if existing cabling is undocumented, does not follow an obvious color code and number scheme, or is difficult to trace, forget it. You can spend hours trying to use wiring that turns out to be unacceptable. Run new cable and leave the existing wiring in place. If you don't know what it does, don't mess with it.

What operating systems are in use over the enterprise? A VMS-only networking solution is different from one that includes UNIX, MS-DOS, and Macintosh machines. In addition, which versions of each of the operating systems is in use? Ideally all VMS systems should be using the latest (or at least the same) version of VMS; all MS-DOS systems should be using the latest version of MS-DOS. Network drivers, printer support, and other features may differ among different versions of a given operating system. Providing everyone with the same version will simplify your task of networking the various systems.

What cabling system should be used given the availability of existing wiring and the inventory you have made of the various systems to be connected? Among the factors to consider are distances separating work groups, the size of each work group, types of applications that will be used, and types of hardware that will be connected. Actually, a combination of cabling hardware will probably be used. You might install a fiber optic backbone that runs between floors and from building to building, use thin-wire coax to connect the work groups to the backbone, and use twisted pair for the work group attachments. Take into account expected growth as well as the permanence of the current installation.

What building codes and other regulations may affect your planned network installation? Don't overlook fire codes, electrical codes, and associated insurance requirements. Will you be allowed to make openings in walls or ceilings? Are there any special electrical requirements—such as conduit or fire-resistant cable—for the work you propose?

Basic wiring regulations are contained in the National Electrical Code, published by the National Fire Protection Association (Batterymarch Park, Quincy MA 02269). You can purchase a copy of the code from any electrical supply house. However, many local and regional regulations are more strict than the NEC standard. Check with local officials to avoid unforeseen work and expenses.

Is there a limit to the amount of money available for a network? Is it a realistic limit? Obviously you can't plan a network without considering cost, but neither can you design an effective system if you are hampered by unrealistic budget limitations. If money is tight, consider implementing the network in stages, over several budget periods, but work to avoid a networking future that is forever handicapped because of short-term underspending.

Who should assemble and install the system? Can a local deal-er, vendor, or consultant provide a turnkey solution? Are there experienced people inside your company who can direct the pro-ject? Who will perform the physical labor? Will you hire outside installers or can maintenance personnel from your own com-pany be pressed into service to install cables, conduit, and other required physical facilities?

Whatever you decide, someone from within your company should assume ultimate responsibility for planning and directing network construction. Only people who are familiar with your company's wants and needs, and who have a vested interest in success, can be expected to work diligently toward these goals.

Before you hire outside services ask to see a working network installed by the prospective company. The system should be as close as possible to your proposed network. Don't accept without evidence vague assertions that your knotty problems are easily solved.

Should you purchase a packaged solution from a vendor or consul-tant, or should you put together the networking pieces you need a la carte? Be sure to look at the whole picture. It should be relatively easy to add up costs of the networking software and the major pieces of hardware for PCs, VAXs, Macintoshes, and workstations.

Add to that the costs for any bridges, gateways, repeaters, and cable, and be liberal in your cable estimates. Remember, bending cable around corners and hugging walls instead of going directly across a floor takes extra length.

Don't overlook expenses for connectors, terminators, wall box-es, wall plates, punch down blocks, and wiring cabinets. If you are doing the work inside the company you may need to pur-chase tools such as punch down block tools or cable crimpers, for example.

Once you have an idea what individual components of the network will cost, you will be in a better position to evaluate a quoted package price from a vendor or consultant.

How much will it cost to install the hardware? When you accept quotes from outside companies, insist that they separate hard-ware costs from labor expenses and that you get detailed pricing.

Plugging boxes into an existing telephone cable for twisted pair Ethernet may be work that a vendor would include in the hardware price; drilling holes in concrete walls and snaking cable through conduits probably is not.

Be sure that any vendor or consultant proposal is specific about what work will be performed. You should ensure that someone from the bidding company has carefully inspected your site so that they fully understand what is involved in connecting your systems.

Show proposals to an outside installation company or electrician. It might make more sense for you to function as a contractor who subcontracts out the materials and installation elements of the job.

What licenses and fees will be required from operating system or application vendors? In most cases you will have to pay either a per-user charge for attached network nodes that use certain programs or a site license fee for a specific number of users.

Many desktop applications are available in two versions, one for stand-alone operation and the other for networking. The stand-alone versions may not include record locking, node support, and the like. Generally you can upgrade a stand-alone version to a networking version in steps of two or more users.

VAX software, on the other hand, is generally set up for multiple users from the beginning and you usually pay for software based on the system on which it will be installed. Further, there may be additional software modules required for networking support.

Additional software not only raises the cost of your proposed network, but complicates the process by requiring that each system be upgraded with new software. Be sure to include these upgrading cost and time factors in your overall system planning.

You should also consider whether existing hardware will be fully compatible with networking software—communications and applications.

What will it cost to train users on the network? Can training be conducted inhouse by your own staff or will you need the services of outside companies? Will there be associated costs for purchase of manuals and other documentation? Network operation may be only slightly different for some users and applications; however, electronic mail and distributed applications may require some retraining. The time and costs involved for bringing users up to speed on the networked installation cannot be overlooked.

Finally, you should make some cost projections on operating the system after it is installed. The importance of this step depends in part on the size of your network, but all network users should be aware of the continuing costs of operation. This may be an extremely small increment that can be absorbed by individual departments, or, with very large installations, operational costs may require separate budgeting and planning. (See the discussion on operational costs below for some additional ideas.)

NETWORK CABLING

The physical connection to Ethernet can be made with at least five types of cables: thick coaxial, thin coax, CATV (cable television), fiber optics, or twisted pair (telephone wire). Which physical connection is used depends on the type of Ethernet.

METHODS OF TRANSMISSION

There are two broad divisions of Ethernet, baseband and broadband.

Baseband is the most widely used of the two and offers the least expensive and simplest way to transmit information on a wire. It uses the entire bandwidth of the cable, usually as a single digital signal.

Broadband Ethernet uses radio frequency (RF) signals to transmit information between nodes. It is called broadband because of the wide frequency spectrum used to carry information. Like commercial radio and television, which share the atmosphere to transmit multiple frequencies to your receiver, broadband Ethernet shares the frequency spectrum on the cable, so you can add voice, video, telemetry, and other information to the same cable that carries the Ethernet signals.

To receive a particular radio or television signal we use a receiver that can tune to specific frequencies, selecting one transmission from all the others. Broadband cabling systems work in a similar way, with various types of equipment that attach to the network capable of selecting out the signals they need to process.

The main difference between broadband Ethernet and baseband Ethernet is the number of data types that each carries. Whereas RF-based broadband networks can share the medium among an almost unlimited number of information types, baseband cable carries only the Ethernet signals.

CABLE SPECIFICATIONS

Broadband signals travel over CATV cable, which is actually a form of coax cable that is common with cable television installations. If you have cable television in your home or if you are using a video recorder, you have probably seen this type of cable connected to your television.

Thickwire Ethernet is obvious because of the size of the cable. Thinwire and baseband cables are about 0.25-inch thick; thickwire cables may be an inch or so in diameter. As an end-user you may not actually see the thick cable, however, because it is normally used as a network backbone, with smaller cables attaching between your workstation and the backbone.

TWISTED PAIR

An increasingly popular Ethernet cable is the unshielded twisted pair used with standard telephone systems. In a building with a telephone wiring system already installed, this is the easiest and least expensive way to attach networked devices. If you are using unshielded twisted pair cable, the wire that attaches to your workstation will probably look like standard telephone cable, the kind that connects your home telephone to the wall. Figure 7.1 shows a configuration using unshielded twisted pair cable.

Although some systems require a customized telephone-type cable that is actually different inside from the wire you use at home, in all probability the computer connection is using standard telephone cable. There may also be a small box attached between your workstation and the wall jack. The cable from the workstation to the box is probably coax; the cable from the box to the wall is most likely flat telephone wire.

Unshielded twisted pair cable offers the advantage of quick and easy connections that can be changed readily. In most offices the telephone wires that connect individual desks or workstations merge in a wiring closet or patch panel at a central location on each floor. This is probably a star configuration with individual connections radiating out from a central hub like the spokes of a wheel (see Figure 7.2).

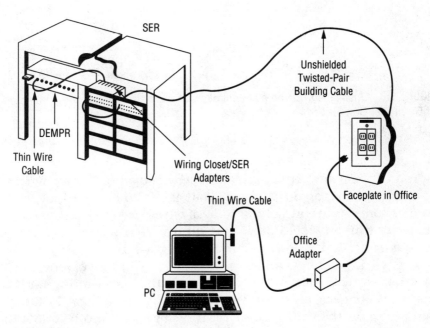

FIGURE 7.1 A twisted pair network can use much if not all of your existing wiring, installed for your in-house telephone system. Thinwire to twisted pair adapters may be required. [Reprinted with permission of Digital Equipment Corporation.]

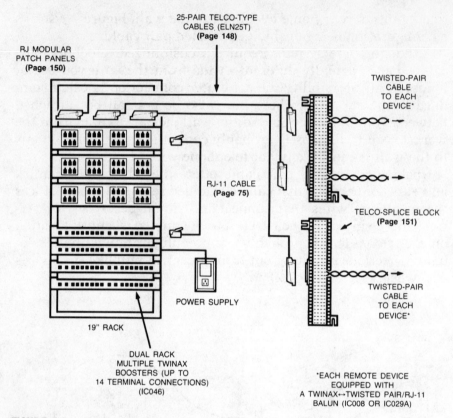

FIGURE 7.2 Unshielded twisted pair central patch panel. [Reprinted with permission of Black Box Corporation.]

You connect into this patch panel by plugging a wire with a modular connector on it into a wall jack. When you make the connection you are attaching to four wires (two twisted pair) or six wires (three twisted pair) that run through the wall, into the ceiling or floor, and to the central wiring location.

This wiring configuration means that if you move your work location you can take your computer with you—simply unplug this wall connection, move the equipment to the new location, and plug into the wall jack there. If changes need to be made to your physical connection to the network, they are made at the central wiring location by moving wires on a punch down block as shown in Figure 7.3, for example.

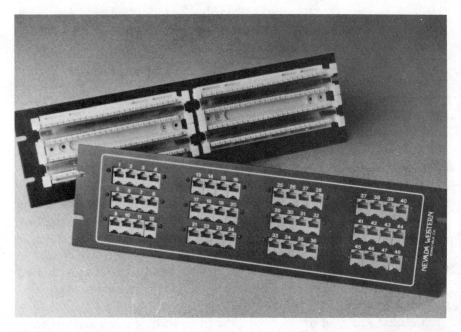

FIGURE 7.3 Telephone company-type punch down block and modular patch panel. [Reprinted with permission of Nevada Western.]

Right now telephone wiring is probably not used as often as coax cable, but it will be. Look for this wiring scheme to become the standard for office- and floor-level connections. For connecting users between floors, coaxial cable is presently the most common—either thinwire or thickwire—but optical (fiber) cable is gaining popularity.

Fiber cable uses laser diodes at either end of the link to transmit information over a light-conducting cable. The advantage to fiber is its small size, large data capacity, and resistance to outside interference. Although standard fiber cable is only a fraction of the size of standard coax, its carrying capacity is hundreds of times greater.

In addition, it is not affected by outside signal sources such as power lines, electric motors, fluorescent lights, and other electrical noise sources. Moreover, wires radiate signals of their own as data are transmitted and this radiation, under certain conditions, can be detected by sensitive receiving devices, which compromises the security of the network. To intercept a fiber transmission, someone must make a physical connection to the network. This makes unauthorized access much more difficult.

The cost of the equipment to convert electrical signals to optical signals is a slight disadvantage to fiber cabling systems at this point. Information is transferred over a fiber cable by modulating an LED (light emitting diode). This technique results in very fast, reliable, and secure communications. However, because computer systems operate with electrical energy—swings in voltage—a conversion device is required at both ends of the link. Price is an obstacle to making the conversion to fiber in some installations, but the cost of such conversion equipment is falling rapidly as an increasing number of companies are providing optical networking equipment. Look for optical cable to become the standard for relatively long-distance connections—between floors and from building to building—while unshielded twisted pair cable will carry the majority of network traffic within a single floor or other relatively small area.

The next stage of evolution is for fiber to bring networking signals directly to the desktop. This step likely won't become common for a few years, but the cost of high-speed workstations and high-end PCs is falling rapidly, and the need for networking is growing. These trends will push the need for fiber's communications speed at the desktop.

FDDI

Fiber at the desktop will become more common with the advent of FDDI (Fiber Distributed Data Interface), a higher-speed fiber optical networking standard. FDDI supports communications network speeds to 100 Mbps over optical cable. Vendors are already installing FDDI-technology optical cable backbones to connect floors in large office buildings or to link multiple buildings in a campus environment. FDDI will quickly become the standard for such links, and FDDIs with speeds of 200 Mbps are not far behind.

FDDI uses a dual fiber optic transmission media and a token ring architecture over distances up 100 kilometers. Such high-speed links between departmental LANs will enable even closer ties among the CPUs within a given installation, increasing the feasibility of true distributed processing where processors of modest capability combine through the network to form a computing environment that is effectively much more powerful than even the sum of its individual parts if they were not connected.

Desktop and deskside machines are destined to figure heavily in this scenario along with more powerful departmental-level and mainframe-class machines. Standard Ethernet LANs, especially those based on a twisted pair (telephone cable) wiring plant, will likely remain the standard for departmental or floor-level computing, while FDDI or other high-speed optical links will be used to interconnect these smaller LANs.

This trend is part of a natural progression to bring ever higher-speed links to the desktop. Many current Ethernet installations, for example, use the 10 Mbps link for inter-departmental communications and slower, serial links to the desktop. As prices for Ethernet equipment decline and users demand increasingly higher-speed connectivity, look for 10 Mbps to become the standard to the desktop with 100 Mbps or faster channels providing the links between departments or other larger groups of users.

DECCONNECT

Digital groups its cable schemes into a general category called DECconnect. The system specifies separate cabling systems for each major type of communications.

Communication Type	Cable
10 Mbps Ethernet	Thin wire
Standard terminal communications to 19.2 Kbps	Flat "office cable"
Voice communications	Twisted pair
Video communications	Coax

Although the full DECconnect standard encompasses switching, controllers, and other technology, the outward manifestation you are most likely to encounter in the office is the distinctive Digital wall plate for multimedia connections (Figure 7.4).

The single box and template may include a couple of telephone-type RJ connectors (with modifications), and a pair of coaxial connectors.

The majority of Digital's new hardware now uses EIA 423-A serial communications over flat-wire cable similar to the familiar telephone cable. Newer terminals and printers contain the modified RJ-type jack so you can plug this flat cable right into the back of the device.

For older equipment, you can purchase adapters that plug into the DB-25 serial connectors and change the jack to an RJ series.

Ethernet can be thickwire, thinwire, or twisted pair cable, or you can use fiber cable as the Ethernet backbone, converting to wire at key terminal points in the network.

NETWORK DISTANCE LIMITS

The distance a signal can travel on a network is limited by the design of the network and the type of cabling it uses. Ethernet

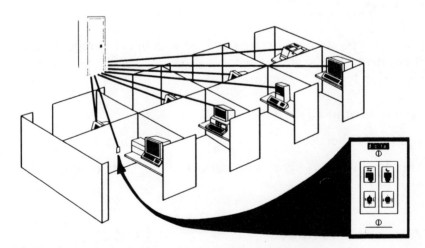

FIGURE 7.4 DECconnect radial (star) topology with Digital faceplate connector. [Reprinted with permission of Digital Equipment Corporation.]

can carry an un-amplified signal about 1,000 feet; a token-ring system is good for about 600 feet. Various devices are available to extend the distance, including:

Repeaters or in-line amplifiers that accept a signal in one side and put it out the other side at a stronger level with no switching or alteration.

Buffered repeaters also amplify the signal, but in addition they can control the flow of signals by issuing "start" and "stop" commands to avoid collisions.

Bridges provide connections between different networks, allowing nodes on either system to work with nodes on the other. Standard bridges do not amplify signals or control their flow, but they can be used with repeaters or they may incorporate repeater components (see Figure 7.5).

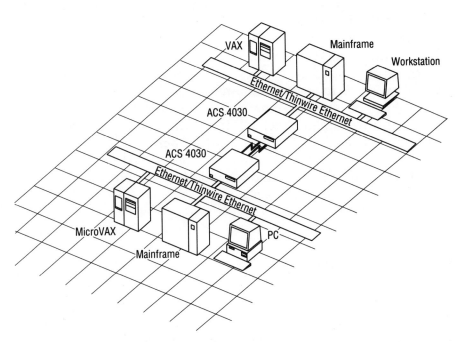

FIGURE 7.5   A remote bridge such as the ACS 4030 can link multiple Ethernet LANs. [Reprinted with permission of Advanced Computer Communications.]

Gateways are intelligent devices that bridge between networks that run incompatible protocols. Gateways work at the OSI session layer to allow nodes on incompatible networks to communicate with each other (see Figure 7.6).

NETWORK OPERATIONAL COSTS

Even if you have done your homework in advance—planning for growth, studying needs, estimating costs—if you are like most network users you will have difficulty getting a handle on costs of network operation.

While not a trivial task, estimating and analyzing costs of network installation is fairly straightforward. With few exceptions network components can be separated and costs identified; the labor costs involved with planning and installation occur over a relatively short time and can be codified.

Once the network is operational, however, ongoing costs get buried within departmental and corporatewide budgets. With a small system the costs of operation aren't large, and it may not be important to analyze them.

With large systems, however, it is more important to keep track of expenses incurred in maintaining computer links. At the same time, you should remain aware of the benefits received for a given investment. After all, if a decision has been made to design and install a network, it must be perceived as necessary, so don't be deterred by the threat of operational expenses. You should be aware of them and provide for regular analysis and cost containment, but that's all.

LABELING COSTS

You can probably identify additional categories for your particular installation, but basically there are two types of costs associated with networking once the system has been installed: ongoing operation, and changes and upgrades.

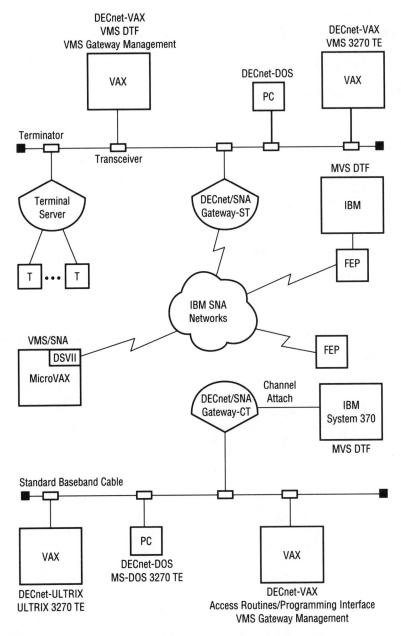

FIGURE 7.6 Gateways allow one type of network communication with an otherwise incompatible network. Digital's DECnet/SNA VMS Gateway is one example of this facility. [Reprinted with permission of Digital Equipment Corporation.]

Within each of these categories, you can probably identify several of the following obvious components:

Ongoing operation

Equipment maintenance

Software maintenance

Software license fees

> Communications

> Terminal emulation

> Utilities and applications

Monitoring and managing the network

Identifying and correcting problems

Training

Administration

Communications

> Line leases

> Dial-up communications

> Satellite links

Facilities

> Office space

> Equipment space

> Wiring closets and storage

Changes and upgrades

Equipment replacement and upgrades

Software replacement and upgrades

Re-configuration

> Adding new users

Moving existing users

Deleting existing users

Building expansion

The precise categories will vary slightly with each installation, but this is a useful general list. Avoid getting sidetracked from the rest of your business responsibilities by trying to analyze every penny spent in each category on a short-term basis. Your planning, projections, and analysis should cover a longer period, say three to five years.

Why? Well, if enough up-front work was done in the first place, you have already justified the cost and effort in designing and installing the network. Enhanced communications facilities are desirable and necessary, and you have already decided to go ahead with the project. At this stage you accept—implicitly or explicitly—that it will cost something to maintain these new facilities. If you assign too many resources to tracking costs, the overall operation will become less efficient.

From a practical standpoint, however, you should have a realistic idea of what it costs to give you these enhanced features. Compare a network to your telephone system. Maintaining a flexible, easily accessible telephone system is an accepted part of doing business. While most businesses periodically check telephone usage for abuse, waste, and inefficiency, few companies conduct ongoing audits of every facet of maintaining voice communications.

The same should be true for your computer network. You should create an awareness among the appropriate staff and establish procedures to study and report findings, but you should not allow the issue of network operational costs to become a consuming, distracting issue.

THE ASSUMPTIONS

One way to begin an evaluation of network expenses is to start with data already collected by other organizations. Your company won't fit precisely into anyone else's profile, of course, but data generated from others experiences can only help.

The Index Group, Inc., a Cambridge-based research and consulting firm, for example, found in a recent study of eleven corporate networking sites that on the average it costs about $3,178 over five years to operate each network node. If you include acquisition costs, the figure is $4,969. These costs were derived by surveying operators of installed networks that ranged in size from 1,155 to 45,000 ports and included IBM as well as Digital as the principal vendor.

In addition to the $635 annual cost per node, the study showed that while there is a relationship between total number of nodes and number of network changes per year, size alone does not dictate how much a configuration will be changed. Figure 7.7 shows corporate network costs for a five-year period.

As you might expect, networks with the largest number of nodes reported more changes than the smaller networks, but the data shows that other factors are obviously at work. One Digital-based network with 40,000 nodes, for example, reported 16,400 changes per year while a 45,000-node IBM network reported only 5,000 changes.

One reason for the differences could be the network topology. The predominantly Digital network in this example is a distributed network while the IBM network is centralized. Addi-

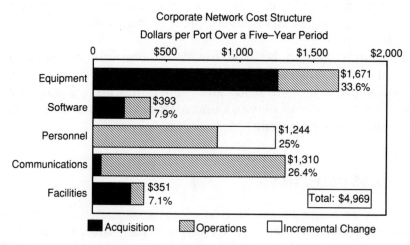

FIGURE 7.7 Five-year network costs. [Reprinted with permission of Index Group, Inc.]

tionally, other factors within each enterprise could affect change requirements.

As a Digital user you will appreciate another finding from the Index Group research: The average per-port cost of a centralized network is more than double the cost of a similar distributed topology.

When you separate centralized and decentralized networks, the study shows a per-port cost, including acquisition, of $6,242 for centralized configurations compared to only $2,741 for distributed networks. The largest saving is attributed to communications line costs, according to the study. While centralized networks required an average of $1,957 (31.3%) per port for communications over five years, the cost for distributed systems was only $179 (6.5%). Figure 7.8 shows a breakdown of corporate network costs comparing distributed and centralized networks.

Finally, notice that the Index Group study showed that a significant part of overall operations cost goes to personnel—in some cases as much as 50 percent of the total (See Figure 7.9).

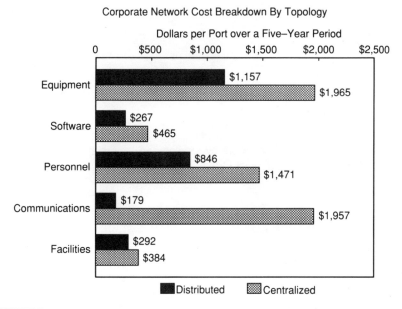

FIGURE 7.8 Five-year network costs by topology. [Reprinted with permission of Index Group, Inc.]

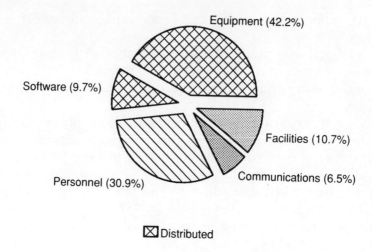

☒ Distributed

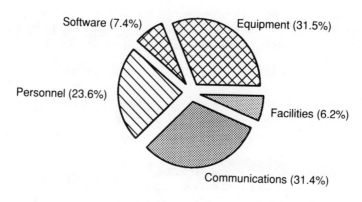

☒ Centralized

FIGURE 7.9 Five-year network costs by topology as a percent of total expenses. [Reprinted with permission of Index Group, Inc.]

CHAPTER SUMMARY

The physical inventory of network components, as well as your individual networking requirements, are important considerations. You must understand these aspects of connecting computer equipment in advance to avoid unnecessary effort and expense.

Try to be expansive in your planning by leaving room for growth, foreseen and unforeseen. Budget more money than seems immediately necessary and spend some of it up front to smooth the way for the future.

Among the factors to be considered are network distance, physical media, software to be used, and hardware to be connected. And don't forget to factor in the long-term costs of network operation because up to two-thirds of the total cost of network ownership can occur after the initial acquisition.

This chapter gives an overview of these factors. Use this information as a starting point for planning your own network or for expanding existing facilities.

The next chapter introduces the concept of PC to VAX communications. With the growth of PCs on the desktop no VAX-to-VAX network planning should ignore PCs and workstations as part of the mix.

PC-VAX
Communications

Just as few VAXs stand alone—one VAX frequently talks to other VAXs—few PCs stand alone in corporate computing environments. Although PC users initially turned away from host computers to regain control over their own computers, they are now looking for host and PC-to-PC connectivity.

One VAX or a group of connected VAXs provide a good platform to give these PC users what they want. This chapter discusses some aspects of PC-to-VAX communication from the VAX perspective.

THE VAX PERSPECTIVE

Almost all VAX computing environments include at least some PC or Apple Macintosh hardware. In fact, a survey published by Digital News in late 1989 showed that 51 percent of VAX sites have at least one Macintosh computer while 91 percent are using at least one PC. Even more significant than the raw numbers is the dramatic increase in Macintosh (14 percent) and PC (10 percent) usage from just a few months earlier.

In addition, a significant number of these PCs and Macs are connected to VAXs. Although many sites including some with multiple desktop machines reported that none was connected, most reported plans to provide desktop-to-VAX connectivity.

There are many reasons for allowing—even encouraging—PC and Macintosh users to attach to a VAX host or VAX network.

Check your own operation and it is a good bet you'll discover, or already know, that applications development constantly runs behind demand. The average delay is approximately six months. But by budgeting even $2000 or less, users can purchase a desktop machine and the tools needed to produce many useful applications quickly. Figure 8.1 shows a typical computer-intensive environment.

Moreover, after the hardware is in place, additional software is relatively inexpensive compared to the same application on even a MicroVAX II. Although you may have to pay several thousand dollars per user for VAX application software, a $500 PC software package is considered expensive.

In fact, thousands of highly functional packages are available for under $100—word processing, multitasking utilities, windowing programs, even sophisticated CAD/CAM design packages. For

FIGURE 8.1 In compute-intensive environments such as CAD/Logic simulation or CAE software development, a shared processor such as the MicroVAX 3600 may be chosen. However, more and more Digital environment desktops also include PC-based workstations. [Reprinted with permission of Digital Equipment Corporation.]

example, Microsoft Windows, one of the user interface standards among PC users, is readily available for about $80 from many suppliers.

While Digital sells third-party VAX windowing tools for $1,200 to $14,000, user pressure and intense competition has forced companies to sell their PC software for one-tenth or less of the original price. At these reduced prices you still receive professional documentation and aggressive company telephone support, in most cases.

Another good reason for letting PCs take on some computing tasks is the compute power they provide to individual users. Terminal users attached to a VAX share the power of the CPU with everybody else. This wasn't a problem a few years ago because PCs weren't particularly powerful and there was little applications software for them.

That's not true today. A MicroVAX II, for example, can support maybe 30 users from a hardware standpoint, yet the CPU is capable of only about 1 MIPS (million instructions per second). A 12 MHz 80286 PC is easily a 2 MIPS machine, while the very latest PC technology, a 33MHz 80386, is clocked by most vendors at about 8 VAX MIPS.

These high-end PC machines perform very well as LAN file servers, but they are also used frequently as dedicated, single-user workstations. Once you get used to driving this kind of power all by yourself, sharing a 1 MIPS machine with 30 other users is unacceptable.

And there are benefits from the VAX manager's standpoint to having PCs in strategic locations around the company. They give users who need it a high-speed computing platform while offloading some tasks from the host. Properly designed and carefully placed PC systems are an efficient and cost-effective way to increase the power of your corporate computer resources (see Figure 8.2).

But the central host and its support personnel now have some attractive services to offer the PC user. Desktop computer drivers are discovering the value of connectivity, in being able to share mail and data with others.

ALL ABOUT PCs

The term PC is a generic name for any personal computer, but the original PC was IBM's personal computer and its later models the PC/XT and PC/AT. Hundreds of companies now build PCs that are compatible with IBM's original BIOS (Basic Input/Output System) firmware, disk format, and display protocols, and these new machines are generally faster and have more features than IBM's early models.

IBM has moved from this original, open, desktop architecture to a new line, the Personal System/2 or PS/2. All of the models in this family are faster and have more features than the original PCs. Also, the PS/2s use a new microchannel architecture that is basically incompatible with the original PC bus.

Contrary to the official IBM line that the new bus gives better performance and is a well-defined growth path to future operat-

FIGURE 8.2 Digital's integrated personal computing solutions extend the DEC-net/OSI and VMS to MS-DOS computers. [Reprinted with permission of Digital Equipment Corporation.]

ing systems and applications, one reason they dropped the established bus was to regain control of the desktop business. So far, however, there has been no rising groundswell of support for the new systems. Applications just became widely available during 1989 and millions of users already are firmly established with the older bus which works with existing hardware and software. Moreover, there are so many "clone" computer vendors that competition is providing high-speed hardware at prices IBM can't match with the new PS/2 line.

PC OVERVIEW

Although the first PCs had limited capability because of small memories, little storage, and few applications, that original 1981 design has undergone many revisions and it has been cloned and copied by companies all over the world. The original PC used an Intel 8088 CPU running at 4.77 MHz. Although this is a 16-bit chip, it talks to the outside world over an 8-bit bus.

This PC consisted of a horizontal main board—frequently called the motherboard—and sockets for up to five vertically mounted adapter cards. The motherboard holds the microprocessor and its associated chips including an optional math coprocessor, the BIOS and other firmware, an integral bus (backplane) with connectors to hold expansion modules, bus interface circuitry, and a real-time clock. Rear-panel connectors bring in AC power and attach a video display and a Centronics parallel printer.

A case with fan, power supply, and room for up to two full-height, 5.25-inch storage devices houses the system. The original PC contained dual diskette drives.

Interestingly, very little has changed in this basic physical design over the years. The cases increased in size for a while to hold larger drives, and now they have gotten smaller to provide a smaller footprint, but the basic arrangement of motherboard, expansion slots, power supply, case, and drive slots remains the same.

Although IBM no longer sells this early model, you can purchase the basic design, with some enhancements, from many clone manufacturers. Generally provided in a PC/XT configuration, which has 8 motherboard expansion slots instead of 5, the current version of this machine runs two or three times faster than the original. Other enhancements include motherboard-mounted serial and parallel ports, integral disk controllers, and much larger hard drives.

IBM's first break with the original design was with the PC/AT (for advanced technology). This computer uses an Intel 80286 CPU and remains the most popular in terms of unit sales.

The 80286 is a 16-bit chip capable of 24-bit external addressing. The PC/AT shares physical similarities with earlier models, and consists of a motherboard with room for eight plug-in adapters. The original PC/AT motherboard was larger than the XT model, but many clone vendors offer a "baby" AT with a motherboard that is the same size as the PC/XT, providing XT users a relatively easy way to upgrade their machines.

Some of these smaller-format ATs have room for only five expansion modules, but this is not necessarily a limitation because fewer expansion cards are needed with most of these machines. The first PCs had only 64 Kbytes of system RAM on the motherboard, for example, but the new AT-compatible sometimes have 4 Mbytes or more on the main board.

The next generation PCs use the 80386 CPU. This is a 32-bit device that supports true multi-user, multitasking systems. The 80386 chip forms the basis for IBM's PS/2 offerings and it is the chip of choice among engineering and other power users who require multitasking, graphics, or multi-user operation. Versions of the 80386 chip can be operated to 33MHz, providing a desktop machine with performance that rivals many of Digital's VAX computers. Some of the newer 80386 machines, for example, have been benchmarked at 8 MIPS while a MicroVAX II is rated at 0.9 MIPS. Digital's 3000-family of MicroVAXs range from 2.4 MIPS to 2.7 MIPS.

The price:performance ratio on these high speed 80386 PCs is extremely good. A fully configured 5- to 8-MIPS machine is available for $4,000 to $8,000, a third or a fourth of the cost of a MicroVAX. So why would anyone choose a VAX instead of an 80386-based PC? The major reason is the VAX operating system. The network manager in Figure 8.3 is an example of how PCs can be used in a VAX environment.

VAX VMS is a powerful, multi-user, multitasking operating system that has stood the test of time in real life, online environments. It has consistently been a solid, relatively easy to use, and powerful system in distributed environments for lots of users.

PC OPERATING SYSTEMS

The most common PC operating system, MS-DOS or PC-DOS, has a different legacy. It originated in the days of low-power machines, single floppy drives, and 64K memory systems. Although it has developed over the years to support very large hard drives, memory to 16 Mbytes, powerful CPUs, and networking, it does not support multitasking or multi-user operation.

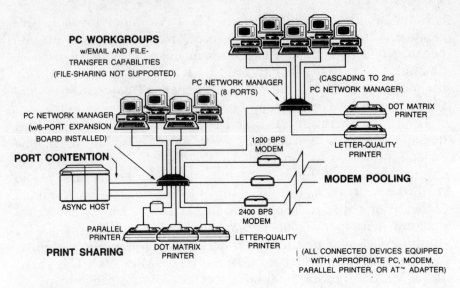

PC WORKGROUPS
w/EMAIL AND FILE-
TRANSFER CAPABILITIES
(FILE-SHARING NOT SUPPORTED)

PC NETWORK MANAGER
(8 PORTS)

(CASCADING TO 2nd
PC NETWORK MANAGER)

PC NETWORK MANAGER
(w/6-PORT EXPANSION
BOARD INSTALLED)

DOT MATRIX
PRINTER

1200 BPS
MODEM

LETTER-QUALITY
PRINTER

PORT CONTENTION

MODEM POOLING

ASYNC HOST

2400 BPS
MODEM

PARALLEL
PRINTER

LETTER-QUALITY
PRINTER

PRINT SHARING

DOT MATRIX
PRINTER

(ALL CONNECTED DEVICES EQUIPPED
WITH APPROPRIATE PC, MODEM,
PARALLEL PRINTER, OR AT™ ADAPTER)

FIGURE 8.3 The PC serial port can be used to access the VAX environment with serial networking products similar to the Black Box Network Manager. File transfer and resource sharing is conducted over serial links at up to 115 Kbaud. [Reproduced with permission of Black Box Corporation.]

IBM's new operating system, OS/2, is intended to offer these big machine services, but it has a long way to go before it provides everything power users need in a multi-user, networking environment. Besides, as a new operating system it lacks the broad base of end-user and system applications already available for MS-DOS and VMS.

Predictions from industry analysts such as IDC in Framingham, MA, show only about 25 percent of installed PCs will be running OS/2 in 1992. Whatever happens to OS/2, there are so many installed 8088 and even later machines running MS-DOS successfully that users are hesitant to switch. A new operating system requires not only third-party support for applications software, but in-house utilities and other applications will have to be rewritten.

Now that the power of desktop PCs has grown, some analysts believe that UNIX has the potential to step in as the multi-user, networked operating system of choice among corporate power users. Although UNIX was not practical on the PCs of a few years ago because they lacked memory, storage, and CPU power, a 80386-based PC can currently run UNIX without difficulty. In fact, some manufacturers have abandoned the 68000 family of processors—traditional UNIX engines—in favor of the 80386 and even newer 80486 processors.

For existing PC users, the same problem plagues UNIX that troubles OS/2. UNIX is not MS-DOS, and those thousands of inexpensive, tried and tested applications won't run on a new operating system. In addition, UNIX is known to be too technical and not particularly user friendly. Even the UNIX shells designed to alleviate that problem have not done a particularly good job of attracting the average user.

That trend may be changing with the new popularity of the X-Window System. Fairly recent standards adopted by OSF (Open Software Federation) and embraced by a number of hardware and software vendors, have prompted development of X-based applications, including "desktop" software environments that tame UNIX and make it a realistic operating environment for just about any PC user.

Whether UNIX and OS/2 takes off or not, for the foreseeable future, MS-DOS and VMS will make excellent cooperative computing partners. MS-DOS provides enough power for the single user at a desktop and it hosts thousands of useful, low-cost applications to drive the hardware. VMS, on the other hand, in conjunction with established and growing VAX hardware, provides an excellent platform for these PC users to share storage, to connect for electronic mail and file sharing, and to have their PC software backed up and upgraded with a minimum of central site effort.

Over the next few years PC-to-VAX communications will take on a new and important role in all computing enterprises that include VAXs. For that reason, VAX-oriented users should become familiar with PC platforms and how they can work with VAXs to provide all users complete computing support.

PC PRODUCTS

There are too many PC products to provide an exhaustive summary of everything available. But much of the PC computing hardware on the market today is based on and modeled after the original IBM design. By understanding the basics of IBM's initial offerings you can adequately judge the breadth of the PC market.

THE ORIGINAL PC

IBM's first machine, the Personal Computer that gave us the generic name PC for all personal machines, was woefully simple and under-powered by today's standards. Strange as it sounds, this machine was configured with ROM-based BASIC, a cassette port for loading programs at about 300 baud, and up to two 5.25-inch disk drives that stored 160 Kbytes of information each. Standard system memory was 64 Kbytes and five expansion slots were supported.

Thousands of these machines are still in use, but most of them have probably been upgraded with more memory and a hard drive. If you want to use one of these old machines in a PC-to-VAX link, plan on upgrading the ROM BIOS. The original machine did not support hard drives and this ancient ROM is most likely incompatible with many communications programs.

PC/XT

The PC/XT added three more expansion sockets and a 10 Mbyte hard drive. The motherboard held up to 256 Kbytes of RAM. For awhile that was enough RAM to run most applications, but later models supplied 512 Kbytes of RAM on the system board.

As late as 1985 a typical PC/XT configuration would have cost close to $5,000. High-speed third-party clones of the XT are available today with more memory and storage at prices one-fourth to one-fifth of the original.

PC/AT

IBM's Advanced Technology PC, the PC/AT was the beginning of the next generation. Using a 16-bit chip with an 8-bit I/O bus that includes 24-bit addressing, the PC/AT could support up to two "dumb" terminals for a total of three users on a single machine. To maintain compatibility with earlier expansion modules the AT includes some standard 8-bit expansion slots.

Although the PC/AT's multi-user features were highly touted when the machine was released, it never became popular. The original 6 MHz clock speed did not really produce a machine powerful enough for multi-user applications, and MS-DOS is not a multi-user operating system. The PC/AT was supplied with a 20 Mbyte hard disk and introduced the 1.2 Mbyte high-density diskette drive.

PS/2 MACHINES

The first four members of the PS/2 line were announced early in 1987. A number of new models have been released since then, and a few PS/2 clones are in the offing, but the PS/2 line does not enjoy the traditional IBM domination of the desktop market.

The four initial offerings were the PS/2 model 30, model 50, model 40, and model 80. Each machine is also available in multiple configurations. Interestingly, the new line uses an 8086 CPU at the low-end, a mid-range machine uses the 80286 CPU, and 80386 CPUs are used at the high-end. The systems share some common features. All use the PC/AT-style enhanced keyboard introduced in 1986. With the PS/2 line, IBM broke away from the 5.25-inch diskette drive in favor of 720 Kbyte and 1.44 Mbyte, 3.5-inch diskettes.

The PS/2 line (with the exception of the model 30) use IBM's 32-bit microchannel bus designed to provide the bandwidth necessary for new high-speed applications.

Although IBM has not released an 80386-based machine that retains the original PC bus architecture, many third-party manufacturers have. IBM's 80386 32-bit machines are designed around a new microchannel bus in the PS/2 line. Other manufacturers have chosen not to abandon the existing bus, so 80386 machines usually have a single, proprietary 32-bit memory expansion bus and a mixture of PC/AT- and PC/XT-compatible expansion slots.

DIGITAL PCS

So far Digital has not been particularly successful in the PC marketplace. The Digital Rainbow and Professional lines were introduced in the early 1980s, and although both families offered good technical quality and design, neither did well commercially. Until early 1989 Digital's public policy was to concentrate on ways to connect personal computers to the Digital computing environment through networking tools instead of to develop its own PC line. There was a hint of change in Digital's strategy in the fall of 1988 when president Kenneth Olsen stated publicly that his company "will never make our own PC line. We may sell someone else's."

A few months later, on January 10, 1989, Digital announced an agreement with Tandy Corporation to market a modified version of Tandy's high-end 80286 and 80386 PCs. The DECstation line included a 10 MHz 80286 model (DECstation 210), a 16 MHz 80386 (DECstation 316), and a 20 MHz 80386 (DECstation 320). Although Tandy is making the PCs for Digital—essentially off-the-shelf 3000 and 4000 models—the company has made some significant modifications to the design to enable the Tandy PC to work with existing Digital network interfaces. Digital has also secured the right to manufacture the machines using the Tandy design, if such a move becomes economically feasible in the future.

A similar agreement with Olivetti allows Digital to offer PCs to its European customers. The Olivetti could generate $200 million for the company during 1990, industry observers believe. Digital is marketing other products such as the VAXstation 3100 shown in Figure 8.4.

It is all part of Digital's overall company philosophy of distributed processing and networking. You can buy PCs that do more for less money than the Digital/Tandy models, but many companies obviously will opt for the new DECstations for a number of logical reasons:

To maintain a single source for all computing hardware. In a Digital-only shop this is a valid consideration.

To ensure communications compatibility with existing or about-to-be-purchased networking hardware and software.

FIGURE 8.4 In addition to traditional PCs from Tandy, Digital is selling workstations, such as the VAXstation 3100, that bridge the gap between PCs and full-sized VAXs. VAXs of all sizes are destined to co-exist with PCs in the Digital marketplace. [Reprinted with permission of Digital Equipment Corporation.].

Digital has modified the Tandy PCs it sells to work flawlessly with its own network interface cards and communications software. You can make these devices work with third-party PCs, but the road might be a little longer or a little rougher.

To secure vendor service for the full complement of computer hardware, including PCs. By purchasing PCs from the same source as other computer resources, maintenance should be easy to arrange.

In addition, existing quantity discount arrangements apply to the PCs. The PCs are available through standard Digital distribution channels, including DECdirect catalog and the online DEC-store.

So far, Digital is supporting only SCSI (small computer system interface) devices for the Tandy machines in capacities to 170 Mbytes. In addition, a 150 Mbyte, one-quarter inch, QIC-150-compatible tape drive is available. The standard video devices are VGA-compatible interface boards and displays.

Configurations from basic units that include only a single 3.5-inch, high-density diskette drive and keyboard (Basic Configuration), through high-end packages with Ethernet adapters, color monitors, and multiple storage devices, are available. The standard packaged system includes a VGA-compatible interface, a monochrome monitor, the MS-DOS operating system, and a one-year, return-to-Digital warranty.

The PCs are compatible with Digital's existing PC networking products, including the DEPCA Ethernet adapter and VMS services for MS-DOS software discussed later. In addition, MS-DOS DECwindows software gives PC users the same applications interface as workstation users.

The PC version of DECwindows lacks the multifunction capability of the workstations, but users still can access DECwindows applications residing and executing on other systems in a network, and display computed results on their local PC screens.

The changes Digital has specified in the original Tandy design ensure ease of integration into an enterprise-wide environment through networking. For example, the I/O drivers available through MS-DOS and onboard ROMs have been modified for compatibility with Digital's serial port protocols for printers.

Digital printers use XON/XOFF software handshaking protocol (Control-S/control-Q); many PC devices use hardware data terminal ready (DTR) and data set ready (DSR) protocols. With the changes, standard PC functions are supported and users can change serial port operation through the SETUP utility or with Digital's modified version of the DOS MODE command. Figure 8.5 shows Ethernet interface cards, giving PCs access to Ethernet.

Significant firmware changes for the Tandy SCSI interface were required for compatibility with network interface cards. Such changes are relatively common when interfacing disk drives, network interfaces, and other I/O devices simultaneously in PCs to avoid conflicts among various hardware and software interrupt routines. Many PC interfaces include switches or jumpers to make these changes.

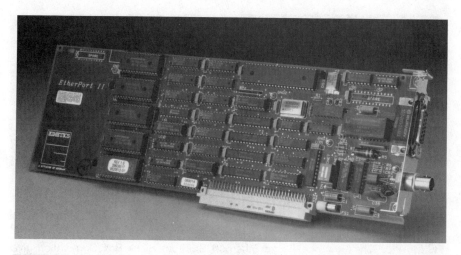

FIGURE 8.5 Ethernet interface cards for the PC bus, such as the 5010E and 5210E from Black Box Corporation, give PCs access to Ethernet. With the proper interface software, PCs can become end node members of a DECnet enterprise. [Reproduced with permission of Black Box Corporation.]

None of these changes interfere with normal PC operation with third-party PC-compatible hardware or software, according to the company.

ALL ABOUT THE MACINTOSH

Although Apple Computer's Macintosh line doesn't have the installed base of PC-compatible machines, the Macintosh is, nevertheless, a forceful influence in the VAX world.

Macintosh users can access VAXs in a number of ways (see Figure 8.6). A direct serial link (RS-232C or RS-422) with terminal emulation software is the simplest way, and among the most popular. Apple and other vendors sell Mac-to-VAX communications software. AppleTalk users get a tighter, more integrated link to the VAX with AppleTalk for VMS.

This product brings the VAX into the AppleTalk network and the Macintosh into the DECnet environment. A VAX/VMS application appears as a node on the attached AppleTalk network.

FIGURE 8.6 The Etherport II and Etherport SE from Black Box Corporation give Macintosh users access to Ethernet. [Reproduced with permission of Black Box Corporation.]

A Macintosh node can exchange information with the VAX host and its application. In addition, the Macintosh running as part of an AppleTalk network can access such VAX facilities as DECnet network services, applications software, or large disk storage.

AppleTalk-to-VAX products are also offered by Alisa Systems, Inc. and Technology Concepts. CommUnity-Mac from Technology Concepts, like its counterpart CommUnity-DOS, is software that interfaces with DECnet through an Ethernet controller installed inside the Macintosh. Alisa's TSSnet software operates over asynchronous communications lines or with a Mac-based Ethernet controller.

MAC OVERVIEW

The original Macintosh set the stage for graphical user interfaces on PC-level workstations. Originally designed to appeal to beginning computer users who might be intimidated by cryptic command line interfaces, Apple's GUI has become popular among users at all levels.

Apple's networking architecture, AppleTalk, is included as a standard feature of all Macintosh computers and includes both protocol handling and physical connectors. This was a forward-looking design, but it was limited by offering plug-and-play connections only in the Apple world.

In the mid-1980s, Apple realized that business success for the Macintosh depended on its ability to connect to other types of computers.

APPLETALK ARCHITECTURE

AppleTalk provides full network services including file servers, printer sharing, and multiple media options. AppleTalk was based on the OSI model and the company has pledged to stay compatible with OSI in the Apple future.

Apple has garnered support for AppleTalk in multivendor network environments by providing tools and AppleTalk protocol suites for several non-Macintosh systems. Several third-party vendors use these Apple products as the basis for their networking products.

MACINTOSH PRODUCTS

The Macintosh started as a single, low-powered product, but has evolved into a family of desktop computers for a variety of applications. There are two basic lines: the Macintosh Plus and SE models, which are monochrome, small screened machines that can be expanded to include hard disks and other enhancements, but are basically single-unit machines; the Macintosh II line, which is a bus-based product that can be enhanced in much the same way as the competing PC line.

MAC PLUS

The Macintosh Plus is the successor to the original Mac and is not the entry-level machine. It includes a 9-inch monochrome display, an 800 Kbyte microfloppy disk, a mouse, AppleTalk ROM software, a SCSI port, and four-voice sound. It can be expanded up to 4 Mbytes of RAM.

MAC SE

This midrange Macintosh is designed for business applications. It is built on the Plus platform, but also includes either a second floppy or hard disks to 40 Mbytes. A single expansion slot supports such additions as an MS-DOS co-processor, communications cards, networking cards, and other devices.

MAC II

The Macintosh II uses a more powerful Motorola 68020 processor instead of the smaller machine's 68000. The Mac II can accommodate up to 8 Mbytes of internal RAM on the motherboard. It is the first color Mac and the first of the family not to include an integral display. In addition to the standard Mac operating system, the Mac II can run MS-DOS and UNIX.

This newest Mac looks like an IBM PC and contains six expansion slots. One slot holds the video adapter, leaving five free slots. Hard drives to 80 Mbytes are available.

MAC IIX

A high-powered version of the Mac II line, this machine uses a Motorola 68030 CPU running at 15.7 MHz for a 10 to 15 percent performance improvement over the original Mac II. Essentially the same expansion and storage options fit this machine as the earlier release.

CHAPTER SUMMARY

Recently published surveys show that most VAX sites use either Macintosh or IBM PC-compatible machines. Interestingly, the majority of these desktop machines is not attached to a VAX host. In the Macintosh world, particularly, users seem to be running mostly stand-alone applications. However, users at all levels indicate an interest in connectivity and most are working on plans to bring PCs and Macs into the VAX world.

This chapter gives you an overview of solutions proposed by Digital and some other vendors for connecting desktop machines. There are many more choices in the marketplace—far too many to adequately cover in this book—but as you add PCs or Macs to your VAX operating environment, be sure to investigate connectivity support for them. Incorporating desktop users into the VAX working environment provides these users access to mail, centralized backup, applications, and data that need to be shared throughout the enterprise. In addition, connecting all of the CPUs in a corporation gives MIS personnel better control over applications and makes it easier to coordinate hardware and software upgrades.

Other Communications Environments

Networking in the digital environment means DECnet, communications software that (usually) runs over Ethernet. For the most part, DECnet provides network-level connections among VAXs. Users who access a local VAX host through a terminal server, terminal emulator, or other device also have access to other VAX nodes on the network if they have been given the proper user rights.

Access to Ethernet and the flexibility provided by DECnet and related protocols open up other connection possibilities, especially from the ever popular PC platforms.

PC-RELATED PRODUCTS

Digital's long term philosophy of interactive computing and distributed processing supported by strong networking brought the company naturally into PC-oriented computing as technological advances became available.

The technical pieces required for this transition have been developing for a few years. Now that 8 MIPS, 32-bit PCs are available for under $5000 and are supported by sophisticated applications including PC-to-host communications software, the social reasons for ostracizing PCs from the minicomputer environment are gone.

Digital has traditionally supported the desktop environment through its DECnet Ethernet protocol, PC Ethernet adapters, and applications software. With the new line of PCs from Tandy, Digital continues to upgrade its communications offerings for these and other PC-compatible computers. Figure 9.1 shows the integrated PC network provided by Digital products.

Novell Corp., makers of the NetWare networking products, reports that at least 90 percent of the Fortune 500 companies who have VAXs want to use them as PC LAN servers. Among the applications cited in the study are the following:

- Access departmental and corporate VAXs from PCs without requiring users to learn VAX system commands and procedures.

- Use a VAX platform for secure and stable storage of PC data. Because the VAX hard disks are backed up regularly,

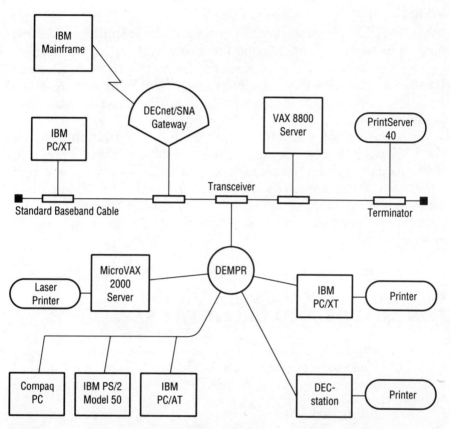

FIGURE 9.1 Digital hardware and software can work together to integrate PCs into a heterogeneous Digital network. [Reprinted with permission of Digital Equipment Corporation.]

PC data stored there is more secure than when it is scattered around the company on PC hard disks.

- Transfer data from PC to VAX and from VAX to PC at network speeds.

- Provide a common LAN environment for personal, work group, departmental, and corporate computers to make it easier to share information transparently from application to application and from computer to computer.

Novell and other companies report that the majority of PCs that are attached to VAXs today are still used with terminal emulators. In this configuration, PC users log on to the VAX as if they were using a conventional terminal. While they can still exchange files, this requires users to understand how VMS and other VAX facilities work. Of course for some applications, this continues to be the most economical and best suited solution.

Digital's PCSA software suite, coupled with Ethernet interface hardware, connects PC users into the VAX environment. Novell's NetWare LAN operating system can also be used in a similar arrangement.

Both solutions go beyond simple terminal emulation, making the VAX hosts on the network appear as PC peripherals for hard disk storage, printer services, and mail, for example. A direct Ethernet connection provides higher speed than a dial-up link, and since 80 percent of new VAX systems have Digital Ethernet controllers installed, using Ethernet as the PC link can also be economical.

DIGITAL'S VAX/VMS SERVICES FOR MS-DOS AND DECNET/PCSA

This is Digital's classic PC-to-VAX connectivity solution. VAX/VMS Services for MS-DOS is the VAX-based or "server" component of the system and DECnet/PCSA is the PC-based or "client" component.

GENERAL FEATURES

VMS Services sets up any VAX as an application, data, and resource server to personal computers. DECnet/PCSA (Personal Computing Systems Architecture) gives the PC DECnet support in conjunction with an Ethernet interface from Digital or a third-party. PCs attached to DECnet with DECnet/PCSA are treated as DECnet peers with other systems on the network. So PC users can store and retrieve files from designated VAX servers, use the printer resources of these systems, and even run PC-based applications directly from networked servers. In addition, PC users can communicate with each other or with users of local and remote servers anywhere on the network.

As PCs become more important in the overall corporate structure, this type of PC-to-VAX architecture gains stature. Earlier PC solutions only allowed the desktop machines access to a local host; any remote activity was conducted through bridges or gateways. VMS Services products enable PCs to participate more fully in the overall networked environment.

CLIENT SOFTWARE

The client portion of this system—the part of the software that runs on the PC—includes Microsoft's MS-Windows user interface, network management tools, terminal emulators, and other software utilities. The server component—the software on the VAX—interfaces the VAX and the PC. Currently the VAX license for VMS Services is included with the DECnet license. Figure 9.2 shows the DECnet-DOS configuration.

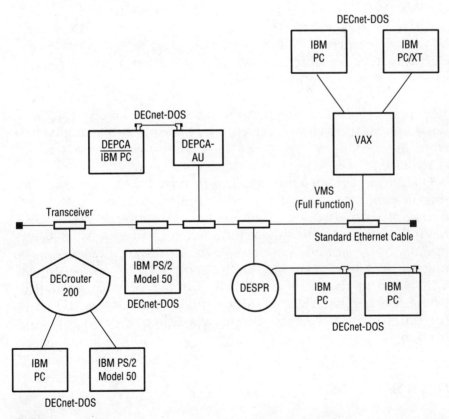

FIGURE 9.2   DECnet-DOS configuration. [Reprinted with permission of Digital Equipment Corporation.]

To get the PC component you can purchase any of the following products:

- Client software to use with existing facilities.

- A Digital Network package that includes PC Ethernet hardware and the PCSA client software.

- A MicroVAX PC Integration package. This includes the server software license, network hardware, and three client licenses.

- The PCLAN/Server 2000.

Once the system is installed and the software loaded, PCs access the designated VAXs in the system as if they were local disk drives. MS-DOS allocates drives A: through F: as local devices. You can assign G: through Z: to remote devices. With VMS services, for example, you could access one VAX system by specifying drive G:. This VAX may hold MS-DOS and other utilities; H: could store one class of application; I: another group of applications or data services, and so on.

These are "virtual" drives that actually represent portions of VAX disk drives. Each virtual drive can reside on separate VAX hosts, or multiple virtual drives can be mapped to a single host. How the system is configured depends on your own DECnet network and the PC applications you are using.

Once you have an Ethernet card in your PC, you can use this link in conjunction with terminal emulation software to logon to any of the networked hosts in the conventional ways. DECnet/PCSA includes terminal emulation software for VT-220 terminals. You could also use any of the third-party terminal emulation packages available for the same job. Of course, to run VAX-based applications the PC users must be assigned appropriate user rights. The emulator support permits each PC user to establish multiple host sessions via Ethernet or a serial connection.

DATA SHARING

Because data files and programs are stored on central servers, PC users can share files simply by specifying the appropriate virtual drive and loading the file through a PC application. If the software supports multi-user applications, multiple users can execute the same application and work with its files simultaneously.

VAX-based MS-DOS files are stored as 512 Kbyte RMS streams or sequential fixed-length records. When a PC user requests one of these files, PCSA software makes the necessary conversion to PC format. VAX-based users access these files directly because they are stored in native VAX format.

This may not be as useful as it first appears. Even though a VAX user can access the physical file, the structure of the information may not be in a form that will be useful. You could type a database file, for example, or maybe even modify it with a VAX editor. It is doubtful, however, whether you could access the database as a data file from a VAX database application. And if VAX users change an MS-DOS file with an application other than the one that created it, file corruption could result.

However, there is a growing number of products that support both VAX and PC platforms. The WordPerfect word processor, for example, operates on the PC and the VAX. Files created in either environment can be used on the other system as if they had been created there.

You can use PC DECnet to create virtual VAX disks 360 Kbytes (equivalent to a standard, double-sided, 5.25-inch PC diskette), to 32 Mbytes, the largest disk MS-DOS can access prior to Version 4.0. You can manage these disks from the PC or from a terminal on the host.

REMOTE BOOT SUPPORT

One interesting feature of Digital's package is the remote boot capability. If you use Digital's own DECnet interface for PCs (a DEPCA board), then diskless PCs can be used as network members. When the PC is turned on, MS-DOS software is automatically downloaded over the network.

The advantage of diskless network nodes is that you save the expense of disk drives for individual PCs. The disadvantage is that every remote-boot PC is totally dependent on the integrity of the network and at least one attached host. If the host should be down for maintenance or any other reason, the local PC will not function.

Another disadvantage is that all applications and data must be stored on a host drive and transferred over the network anytime it is accessed. This increases network traffic and can slow down PC applications.

PCLAN/SERVER

One way to get from the PC environment to a VAX is through a local area network. Multiple PCs connected in a departmental network can access a VAX host through the local server.

Digital's PCLAN/Server 2000 is the company's proprietary LAN based on DECnet and the MicroVAX 2000 desktop computer (see Figure 9.3). Digital estimates that the average PC LAN has 10 nodes and as applications develop these users need access to a host machine. Basing the PC LAN on DECnet can make the transition to the host link somewhat easier, although there are gateways and overlay software that can achieve the same purpose.

In mid-1989 Digital released an upgraded version of its PCLAN product, the PCLAN/Server 3100 (see Figure 9.4). With this packaged server configuration you can service up to 48 PCs through

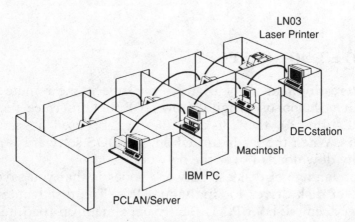

FIGURE 9.3 Work group PC LAN daisy-chain configuration, using PCLAN/Server 2000. [Reprinted with permission of Digital Equipment Corporation.]

FIGURE 9.4 The standard PCLAN/Server 3100 comes with 8 Mbytes of memory, 104 Mbytes of storage, and a 95 Mbyte streaming tape. The packaged system also includes VAX VMS Services for MS-DOS and DECnet/PCS client software. [Reprinted with permission of Digital Equipment Corporation.]

local and wide area networks. This server is based on newer Digital technology, the 3000-series CMOS chip set. You can configure the PCLAN/Server 3100 with up to 312 Mbytes of storage and 32 Mbytes of RAM.

You can connect a PC to a VAX in a number of ways. The physical link can be either direct connect or dial-up serial lines, or Ethernet carrying one of Digital's supported protocols. Digital and a number of third parties provide hardware and software to support the PC-to-VAX solution.

VAX/VMS Services for MS-DOS, the VAX-based server, and the PC-based client component DECnet/PCSA (personal computing systems architecture), form Digital's classic PC-to-VAX connectivity solution.

VMS Services allows any VAX to function as an application, data, and resource server to a large group of personal computers. DECnet/PCSA provides DECnet support for the PC when used with a Digital or third-party Ethernet card.

DECnet/PCSA nodes are treated as peers with other attached systems. That means the PC user can store and retrieve files from VAX servers, use network printer resources, run PC-based applications stored on networked servers, and communicate with users anywhere on the network.

The client portion of this system includes Microsoft's MS-Windows user interface, network management tools, terminal emulators, and other software utilities. The server component provides the interface between the VAX and the PC.

After the host and PC components are loaded, the PC user accesses one or more VAXs in the system as if they were local disk drives. These are virtual drives that actually represent portions of VAX-based disk drives. Each virtual drive can reside on separate VAX hosts, or multiple virtual drives can be mapped to a single host.

In addition, PC users can use the DECnet attachment to logon to any of the networked hosts in the conventional ways. VT-terminal emulation software is included as part of DECnet/PCSA.

Of course there is increasing third-party support for the Digital connection as well. It would be impossible to note every contender for the VAX link, but some of the major players are summarized in the following discussion.

NETWARE

Novell, Inc. is among the premier suppliers of PC-based local area network software that works with a variety of server platforms (see Figure 9.5). The company claims more than 1.5 million NetWare workstations, supported by at least 1,200 vendors, and 4,000 applications are in operation.

Early in 1988, Novell announced NetWare for VMS, software for VAX hosts that gives NetWare-based PC LANs access to the VAX environment by permitting single PCs or PC networks to access VAX hosts as netware servers. Once they are connected

NetWare for VMS Network Support

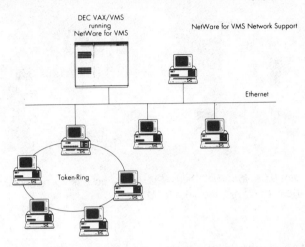

FIGURE 9.5 NetWare for VMS supports PCs directly connected to Ethernet and the VAX, or LAN work groups using other topologies that need access to a VAX host on the network. [Courtesy of Novell, Inc., Provo, UT]

to the VAX, NetWare users can also access other system resources, including high-speed printers or plotters, or remote VAXs connected to the primary server through DECnet.

You can access files and network services noticeably faster from a Novell PC host than from a VAX host—about twice as fast—but operation is still rapid enough to appeal to users of, say, a 9600 baud serial link.

In addition, Novell provides terminal emulation facilities to enable LAN-based PCs to log on to the VAX as if they were VT-series devices, and to operate normally in that environment. In this configuration the PC functions as a VT-class terminal directly attached to the VAX, even though it may actually be at a remote location, accessing the VAX over DECnet and NetWare (see Figure 9.6).

Novell calls its approach to PC connectivity "PC-Centric" because of the heavy emphasis placed on the PC platforms. Although facilities of NetWare for VMS are similar to the Digital PCSA package, Novell claims faster performance over PCSA 2.2. Novell approaches the problem from the desktop perspective

NetWare VMS Remote Support

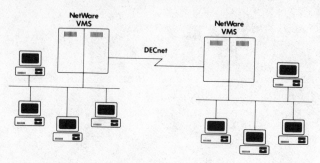

FIGURE 9.6   NetWare for VMS gives PC users access to remote resources via DECnet. Courtesy of Novell, Inc., Provo, UT]

because "the desktop computer is fast becoming the center of computing resources, the focus of applications development, and the window through which end users will see their corporate computing resources. This perspective recognizes the fact that PC users want to access information on minicomputers and mainframes as if the information were on PCs, so that familiar PC commands and programs can be used," as stated in Novell technical literature.

NetWare for VMS runs as a single process on the VAX. It needs a minimum of 2 Mbytes of memory and about 3,000 blocks of disk space. You can use a Digital or Digital-compatible Ethernet card to make the physical attachment of the PC to the network. NetWare for VMS can work alongside other protocols, including LAT or DECnet, but it doesn't use them directly.

The included terminal emulation service (TES) lets you access traditional VAX services over the network. With these facilities VAXs and PCs can easily exchange mail and share files. Transferring files is as simple as entering a PC/MS-DOS copy command.

Using the NetWare shell on the PC, users access the VAX as if it were another local disk drive. You can map up to 26 different drive letters to directories on the VAX, either on the same drive or on different hosts running NetWare for VMS. NetWare files are stored on the VAX in RMS format. They are converted to PC format as they are accessed by the PC. VAX users and PC users can access NetWare files.

If you are using software that runs in both environments you can enjoy full and near-transparent data sharing across the two platforms. VAX WordPerfect users, for example, can create any word processing file they like and users attached to the network with PCs can load them as if they had been created on the PC.

You can even access remote networks from a single PC if there is a DECnet link between the two VAX installations and NetWare for VMS is running on both hosts. Security operations, including account management, file access, queue control, and passwords, remain under the control of the VAX system manager.

For PC users frustrated over computing isolation—not being a part of the corporate network—Novell's VAX-based NetWare is a reasonable solution. The user-friendly PC workstation provides the best of both worlds—the large disk, high-speed printers, electronic mail and other services of the VAX.

Because VAX system personnel tend to stand with their backs to the VAX and look out at the rest of the world, they may be a little slower to accept NetWare. They needn't be, however, if Novell's specifications are accurate. NetWare VMS is described in Novell technical literature as a "multithreaded, event-driven process-optimized for file service," and is only active when users ask for file service operations. Otherwise it hibernates and uses minimal VAX resources.

Obvious advantages from the VAX end are the coordination of PC resources, automatic file backup with the main system, and, according to Novell, the increased number of users a NetWare-based system can actually support compared to a stand-alone VAX if the VAX is running with a limited user VMS license. Novell's stated goal is to maintain leadership in network operating systems and to support evolving workstation standards while remaining hardware independent.

COMMUNITY-DOS

CommUnity-DOS software from Technology Concepts, Inc. also uses Ethernet controllers on the PC to access DECnet. CommUnity-DOS comes with a number of applications, including file server, remote file access, virtual terminal, network management, and VAX/VMS mail support. A similar product is available for the Macintosh and other desktop machines. Users of CommUnity software can link their personal computers and UNIX workstations directly into DECnet as an end-node station, providing the following capabilities:

- Remote file access and file transfer, VMS mail integration with UNIX mail for exchanging mail between DECnet VMS and Comm-Unity systems.

- Task-to-task communications for developing distributed applications across multiple operating systems.

- Network virtual terminal to provide remote logon to a DECnet or CommUnity system.

- DECnet network management.

CommUnity systems are compatible with VMS, Ultrix, and RSX systems on a DECnet Ethernet network. At least 35 third-party vendors are licensing CommUnity software for use on their systems, giving third-party equipment users access to the DECnet environment.

REMOTE ACCESS FACILITY (RAF)

Datability Software Systems offers Remote Access Facility software. RAF consists of two basic software components, one for the host and the other for the PC.

Datability is one of the few companies that uses LAT–compatible protocols. Digital's local area transport protocol is the terminal server portion of DECnet. LAT support greatly expands RAF's flexibility and functionality. For example, even without an active host session, a PC user can display Ethernet traffic to determine active hosts and other information. In essence, each RAC PC workstation appears to the host as a terminal server that supports a listing of available services and connections to specified systems.

The terminal server emulation also permits the PC to support sophisticated printer services. The host system can route PC-based software requests for the local printer to a host-attached printer, for example. In addition, with optional software, host-level print requests can be routed to a PC workstation where the local printer is used as if it were attached directly to a standard terminal server, causing the PC to act like a printer server for the host.

INTERCONNECTIONS

Interconnections supplies hardware and software to connect PC and VAX systems running on different networks. Interconnections can integrate TCP/IP, XNS, NetWare, MS-Net, LAN Manager, Ethernet, Token Ring, and other LANs. Products such as this will gain popularity over the next few years because in many companies PC and VAX connectivity has grown in pieces.

Individual departments selected their own solutions for LAN connectivity, many of which didn't include a link to the corporate host or network. Now, with nearly everyone using a terminal or PC, the value of linking everyone on a common system becomes obvious. Bridges and gateways with the proper software can let you attach these disparate LANs into DECnet and its associated VAX hosts.

VAX SUPERCOMPUTER GATEWAY

When your VAX runs out of steam and you need the high power processing provided by a Cray supercomputer, it is time for the Digital VAX Supercomputer Gateway. This is a hardware/software solution. The package is designed to integrate a Cray into a VAXcluster and DECnet environment.

The gateway links Cray Research, Inc.'s Cray-1, Cray X-MP, Cray Y-MP, and Cray-2 systems to any VAXBI bus system (see Figure 9.7). The maximum distance from the VAX to the Cray is 50 feet. But the gateway VAX can be attached to a cluster and/or Ethernet to provide Cray access to other VAXs in the network or cluster.

FIGURE 9.7 The Digital supercomputer gateway lets VAX computers access Cray supercomputers through a high speed bus connection. Other nodes on the network can use the VAX with the gateway installed to reach the Cray as well. [Reprinted with permission of Digital Equipment Corporation.]

The gateway provides the following features:

- Up to 24 Mbits data transfer between the memory in the gateway VAX and the Cray.

- Ethernet and cluster attachment of additional VAXs.

- Multiple gateways on the same Cray for additional throughput and the extra reliability of redundant systems.

- Diagnostic software on the VAX that can communicate with diagnostic software on the Cray.

REMOTE DIAGNOSTICS COMMUNICATIONS

One important feature that linking VAXs and other computers offers is the ability to conduct hardware and software diagnostics and some maintenance from remote locations. Companies can establish their own dial-up or network links to analyze remote systems, or outside firms can be contracted to do it for you.

Although the technology for remote diagnostics is readily available, only a small minority of third-party maintenance companies that offer service to Digital systems have remote diagnostic capabilities.

Remote diagnostics and data base analysis can be purchased as part of an overall service and maintenance plan from some vendors, however. Digital maintains a hardware and software system based on artificial intelligence technology that can help its service customers predict equipment failures and measure ongoing performance. Data collected at a user site can be accessed remotely and compared against a data base maintained at one of Digital's Customer Support Centers (CSCs).

As shown in Figure 9.8, VAXsim Plus is the diagnostic and expert system software installed on customer hosts. Among its capabilities are monitoring disk performance, predicting a possible failure, conducting automatic backup onto a shadow volume, and shutting down the failing drive. The system requires VMS volume shadowing and another backup disk must be available.

Software problems detected with VAXsim Plus usually can be corrected remotely. Predictive hardware analysis helps Digital

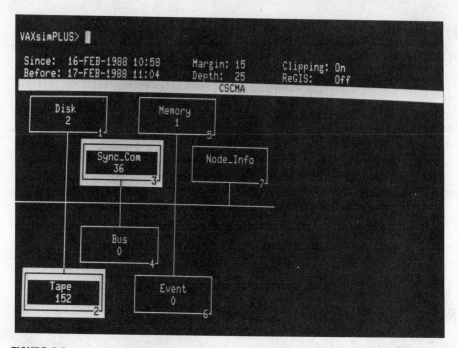

FIGURE 9.8 Monitoring total system performance to assure availability is one of the many functions of VAXsimPLUS. [Reprinted with permission of Digital Equipment Corporation.]

coordinate parts replacement with customer representatives, frequently avoiding downtime caused by equipment failure.

According to figures Digital maintains on its maintenance calls, about 80 percent are software-related. Of those calls some 85 percent are corrected remotely within an hour.

The Digital package can upload and download data between the customer CPU and computers at a CSC if necessary, but the customer is always involved in the process.

If you include network support in a Digital maintenance agreement, the company can install a specially-equipped VAX site processor at your location. The VAX and its associated software monitor error conditions and system performance, building a data base of information that can be used by field service or CSC personnel to diagnose and correct problems.

Electronic Service Specialists Ltd., a Bell Atlantic Company, is among the third-party service vendors that offer remote diagnostics capability. ESS's Rx-Link consists of a dedicated micro-computer system that attaches to the host to monitor system performance and capture system-produced errors. Also included in the standard package is a GE cordless telephone that can be used for technical support calls.

Rx-Link can function as a stand-alone system that automatically dials ESS technical support for diagnosis and problem solving. Alternately, Rx-Link can first alert an on-site operator who can correct the problem locally, call ESS telephone support, and/or download custom diagnostic software for additional analysis.

The ESS system also includes predictive analysis software that can help predict failures before they occur, thereby providing time for corrections or hardware replacements.

Like Digital's remote diagnostic service, ESS uses a central data base as a resource to help track down end-user problems. When an error condition—or a series of conditions—is reported, the central data can be compared against the individual site data to find out if other users have experienced similar problems.

TRW, Inc.'s field service division offers on-demand or scheduled dial-in service for its maintenance customers. Service personnel can log in to a system as a user and run online diagnostics to test peripherals and things that are not critical to the system booting, or they can log in on a scheduled basis as a preventative maintenance measure. In addition, field service personnel can make connections to the main console of the VAX to remotely run stand-alone diagnostics to find faults in systems that aren't bootable.

TRW also develops and markets remote diagnostic software that is being used by a number of third-party service vendors.

Control Data Corporation's engineering service division offers similar facilities to maintenance customers, and like TRW does not support remote uploading and downloading of diagnostic tools or data. Software is installed at the customer site to enable telephone logon for testing and diagnostics. In addition to the software, CDC installs a modem at the customer site.

Dilog in Anaheim, CA is now offering a remote diagnostic option to its government customers, developed at their request. Such services will likely be expanded. The Dilog facility includes circuit boards installed in customer systems to allow service personnel to dial into the system and run diagnostic routines and exercise the system as if it were a console device. The system itself is also capable of reporting failure conditions back to a central service facility. Information can be uploaded and downloaded between the service facility and the customer site. Because Dilog is primarily a hardware maintenance provider, it does not attempt to download replacement software.

Dilog reports that market research on the remote diagnostic option shows "a desire to have it in the rest of the customer base," outside the government-only facilities. The research shows that remote diagnostic facilities can save the provider personnel, time, and money, and the company believes that more and more companies will be offering this capability.

Prognostics, Inc., a Palo Alto market research firm specializing in after market service, calls Digital's remote diagnostic facilities the most sophisticated of all the offerings currently available.

IBM's AS400 system also has some sophisticated capabilities in this area, according to Prognostics. For one thing, persons calling about software questions must now wait for a return call from an IBM technician instead of talking immediately with an IBM expert. This is an effort to motivate customers to use remote uploading and downloading facilities now available.

Hewlett-Packard is also offering some vendor-provided remote facilities, but according to Prognostics they haven't gone as far as Digital in packaging and promoting the service.

One of the problems for service companies is that until recently users have not been particularly receptive to remote diagnostics. Five or six years ago they were basically disinterested, primarily because the capability was viewed as something that helped the vendor do the job better. Now, however, service vendors are emphasizing their ability to do predictive maintenance, changing the approach to one of sharing the responsibility for system maintenance.

Although most users would prefer to have someone fix their machine on-site, more users now accept the fact that remote diagnostics may help the service provider do a faster job. But that capability alone does not sway the customer to the purchase of particular hardware, Prognostics research shows.

At the same time acceptance and awareness has risen dramatically, even among those who initially objected to remote diagnostics, because of security considerations. Security was a much bigger issue when remote diagnostics first came out. Now the concept of outsiders logging into a system, with the proper controls, is apparently becoming accepted.

As diagnostic facilities become more sophisticated, today's reliable hardware will likely approach 100 percent uptime.

CHAPTER SUMMARY

There's more to VAX-to-VAX communications than simply connecting VAXs to Ethernet and running DECnet software. While this Digital-only approach can provide a significant level of improved performance over stand-alone systems, any enterprise looking to broaden host functionality should consider other avenues of expansion.

Especially where PCs and MACs are involved—and what company does not today have a significant number of PCs?—Digital's PCSA or one of the other PC connectivity solutions can be valuable assets. Previously PC users wanted to exist alone and the MIS staff was just as glad to let them operate independently. Today, however, it is to all employees' advantage to bring these personal CPU drivers back into the corporate fold. By linking PCs and VAXs you can enhance backup control, provide better enterprise-wide computer management, make system updates easier, and provide a broader base of applications and data to every user in the company.

In addition, such features as remote maintenance and diagnostic services network management enhance the VAX-to-VAX network.

In the next chapter we discuss the security implications of VAX communications.

Communications Security

Today's computing environment is incomplete without communications. OSI networking standards, X Window System software, and other standards are making all computer platforms accessible to each other, the sum of the parts becoming more powerful than the individual pieces. File sharing, electronic mail, distributed databases, compound documents—all of these features are becoming accepted and expected, even in heterogeneous environments like the one shown in Figure 10.1.

Whatever the application, isolating various computing platforms in an enterprise is all but impossible. Even if no formal interconnectivity policy is established, workstation and PC users have many ways to attach to a VAX. From there it is not particularly difficult to transfer information to another VAX, and

FIGURE 10.1 Few VAXs stand alone any more. From banking to scientific applications, today's system requires communications. Maintaining secure systems is important in every distributed application. [Reprinted with permission of Digital Equipment Corporation.]

another. And it is only slightly more difficult to make a Vax-to-Vax connection.

However good this capability may be for overall computing power and efficiency, it also presents opportunities for abuse, opening the secrets of one system to another. Moreover, as the number of PCs and workstations in a company grows, the potential for theft, damage, and loss increases.

SECURITY PROBLEMS

You may keep the corporate database tightly locked behind the glass walls of the central computer room. Printouts of financial statements, personnel files, and other confidential documents may be carefully locked in steel file drawers.

But look around. The following conditions probably also exist in your company:

- Diskettes are left in desktop PC or Macintosh drives, or stored in plastic cabinets beside operators' desks.

- Corporate personnel files are on a PC hard disk in the human resources department. This machine isn't locked behind secure doors and it may be attached to a departmental LAN.

- Critical corporate data is regularly sent across the country using public telephone lines or outside electronic mail services.

- Internal electronic mail service is available to traveling executives as well as to some of your clients. The dial-in facility is designed to be as friendly as possible to encourage use.

Even if your company doesn't deal with inherently sensitive information—government contracts, competitive product plans, funds transfer or deposit information, medical records, military secrets—the data stored on your various computer systems is instrumental in the operation of your business.

Countless person hours have been spent collecting employee, sales, inventory, financial, and text information. If you were to lose this information, either through theft or carelessness, the cost of replacement in time alone would be considerable.

Your first defense against data loss is a carefully planned back-up procedure. You should include any remote facilities, including PCs and other workstations as part of the back-up procedure. Archived data should be stored away from the main computer installation and another copy should reside off site in another building or in a vault designed for data storage.

A good back-up procedure won't protect your data from theft, but it can help you recover from equipment and software failures, natural disasters, and the most serious threat to data integrity, operator malfunction.

In addition to back-up and data loss considerations, you should implement a set of procedures that do as much as possible—given your situation and resources—to protect information from theft and damage.

LIMITING ACCESS

In a VAX environment like the one shown in Figure 10.2, for example, you have the strength of VMS to help with security issues. The operating system itself includes facilities to establish a secure installation and limit access to various facilities as appropriate. A full discussion of VMS security is beyond the scope of this book, but Digital has a number of useful publications on this topic. Consult the VMS security manual that is part of the operating system documentation set, and consult with your local Digital sales representative to identify publications on VMS security facilities to meet your particular corporate needs.

One key to limiting the risk of unauthorized access is to reduce the number of users that can actually get on the system. For example, if remote users don't need to access the system after certain hours, the modem lines on the VAX can simply be shut off or, better yet, disconnected. A hacker cannot get access to a system if the modem lines are disconnected.

Further limits can be placed on users' privileges, reducing their ability to gain access to the system or to selected parts of the system. Also, where data security is particularly important, you should implement a system of user IDs that make it difficult for outside persons to guess valid IDs.

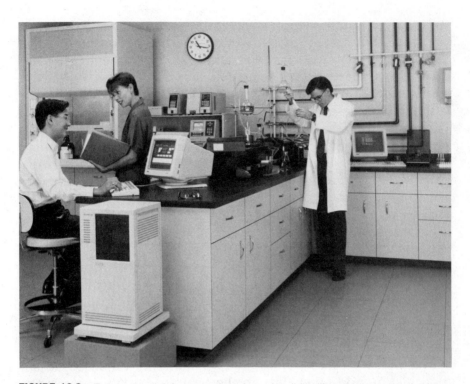

FIGURE 10.2 Even remote laboratory locations, in all likelihood, are networked into the main corporate system. Keeping data secure while making it accessible to appropriate personnel is a delicate balancing act for the MIS manager. [Reprinted with permission of Digital Equipment Corporation.]

For example, in many companies each person accessing the central system uses his or her last name for the logon ID. This is easy for everybody on the network to remember and it makes electronic mail and departmental accounting much simpler than devising another system. However, this convenience extends outside the corporation. If unauthorized people can guess even one or two valid user IDs, they have taken the first step toward breaking into your system.

If employees use last names for user IDs, then guessing valid IDs is relatively easy. All one has to do is secure an inhouse telephone directory, or even simpler, just guess some common names.

To obviate this problem, some users select highly personalized names for themselves—Growler, Tweetypie, Spaceman, or

Iguana. In a small enough organization, if everyone is comfortable with this strategy it can work, though hackers can guess at popular user names as easily as employees' actual names.

For the highest level of security, each user can be assigned a numeric or alphanumeric user ID, possibly tied to department numbers, job description, or sequential node numbers.

The system manager assigns these IDs (Digital calls them UICs for user identification code), and they are stored on the system, along with other information in a user authorization file (UAF). VMS will accept a two part user ID—a group code and a member code—with a total length up to 31 characters. These can be straight numbers such as:

```
1001,2766
1263,0023
```

A numeric user ID is more difficult to remember, perhaps, but it is also more difficult for an outsider to guess.

If you elect to incorporate the user name into the UIC, it is a good idea to add other data to the basic code. You can use the group code to identify a number of persons in a group, or even to specify a group of one, if you need that level of security.

You can tie the group ID to the individual's department within the company, as the following samples indicate; however, this again makes the job of guessing names a little easier.

```
ADMIN,JOHNSON
PAYROLL,SMITH
EXEC,FRANKLYN
```

A more secure ID would consist of group IDs that are not so obvious:

```
GRAPEFRUIT,JORDAN
DATES,EDEN
RAISINS,LYNN
```

You can mix numbers with letters if you set up the files properly, though in an alphanumeric ID scheme the group ID and the user ID must each contain at least one letter.

In addition to user IDs, each person who logs onto the system must have a password. In fact, proper password usage is one of the most important procedures individuals and groups can use to protect corporate data.

Password selection and use involve many considerations. Both personal passwords and system passwords must be implemented to provide an additional level of identification and security. Setting system passwords is a two-stage process using the DCL (digital command language) commands, SET TERMINAL and SET PASSWORD.

After determining the terminals that require passwords, the system manager uses the DCL command SET TERMINAL/SYSP-WD/PERMANENT for each one. These commands are then incorporated into the SYS$MANAGER:SYSTARTUP.COM command which automatically takes care of the setup during system startup. (You can remove these restrictions with the SET TER-MINAL/NOSYSPWD/PERMANENT DCL command.) The system manager can then set a password with the $SET PASS-WORD/SYSTEM command.

The system password should be changed often, at least once a month and perhaps more frequently depending on the size of the system and number of users on the system. The system password should always be changed when a user who knows it leaves the company.

Informing users in advance of setting or changing the system password minimizes login errors. Otherwise users may be denied access either because they don't know the system password or because they are unaware that the terminal they are trying to use requires one.

Suppressing the system announcement is another precaution worth considering. If an unauthorized user wanders into the system, you want to make it hard to identify the system. Also, you don't want curious onlookers to know the system a remote user has dialed up. While this is somewhat dehumanizing, it is a good precaution that requires very little effort.

If your system is small and closed, without remote users, a system sign-on message can be beneficial. It lends an identity to the company, offers a sense of pride and importance to the individual and the company, and is generally a warm greeting for users. However, for medium to large systems, and particularly for open systems (that are accessed remotely), the suppression of the system message is advisable. Use the DEAS-SIGN/SYSTEM SYS$ANNOUNCE command to suppress the system announcement.

One of the easiest methods of limiting access to data and applications lies in a consistent and workable password system. VMS includes procedures for establishing multilevel user rights and passwords. Based on our experience, the majority of installations use only a single level system and then the issue of passwords is taken lightly by most users.

You will find user passwords written down and taped to the side of a terminal, kept in a desk drawer, or placed under the desk blotter. Maybe one-fourth of the users assigned passwords write the password down on the last page of a desktop calendar or enter it in a Rolodex file under "Secret," or even "Password." As discussed earlier, far too many people select passwords that are so simple or obvious that an inventive 10-year-old child could guess them.

A number of generally accepted rules should be followed for choosing and handling both personal and system passwords:

Use a *non-English string of characters* or select words that don't obviously go together. The best password is probably a nonsense word or number, or two words separated by a random non-alphabetic character, CANDY&STREET, for example, or BASE^PLANE.

Use a *password longer than six characters* (the longer the better, but not so long as to annoy users).

Don't choose anything logical or obvious. Avoid parts of a company name or address, a phone number, your name or names of employees, buildings, streets, or dates.

Don't use the same password for all groups, nodes, or services.

Don't store password lists on the computer system.

Don't write down passwords and keep them in obvious places. In the event of an emergency it may be necessary for someone else to access secret passwords, but they should be stored in a secure location with limited access.

Change passwords regularly—at least once a month.

Don't use the same password for multiple accounts or for different services.

Check your regular telephone, electronic mail, communications common carrier, and in-house *bills and statements* of usage. If the list is broken down by time of day or date, inspect each notice for usage during times you know you were not online. Notify the system manager or service coordinator immediately and change your password if you suspect unauthorized usage.

Don't re-enter your password once you are logged on to an account. Some pirates can break into legitimate sessions to issue instructions such as the following example:

Attention. This is the system operator. A computer problem has occurred. Please re-enter your user ID and password now:

If you respond to such a notice you could be handing over your ID and password to an unauthorized user. Instead, sign off immediately and contact the appropriate system administrator.

DES ENCODING COMMUNICATIONS

One way to make a data link secure is to encode information during the transmission process and to store information on disk in an encoded format. There are a number of encoding schemes that can be used over remote lines. One popular encryption technique is DES, the data encryption standard.

DES was developed by IBM and was published as a hardware standard in 1977 by the National Bureau of Standards, now the National Institute of Standards and Technology. DES can also be implemented through software, but software-based DES is typically slower than dedicated DES hardware.

DES consists of two major components, a 64-bit input block, called "plaintext," and a 64-bit output block, called "ciphertext". DES converts plaintext into ciphertext using a 64-bit key (56 significant bits and 8 parity bits). A block of plaintext can be encrypted in 2^56 or 70 quadrillion (about 70,000,000,000,000,000) different ways.

DES offers two primary encryption modes: block and cipher-feedback. Each method has some strengths and weaknesses.

The disadvantage of using block mode is that patterns evolve during the encryption process because the same encryption key is used for each block of plaintext. Therefore, matching plaintext blocks will always yield matching ciphertext blocks. Anyone who has attempted to solve cryptograms in the daily newspaper knows how easy it can be to use patterns to decrypt the message.

The strength of block mode encryption, on the other hand, is that transmissions or encrypted files that become corrupted can still be partially decrypted.

Cipher-feedback mode offers more secure data encryption using a "key stream" based on an initial input chain value (seed) to encrypt plaintext blocks. Each time a block is encrypted a new key is used. In this mode, each sequential ciphertext is a function of the previous ciphertext block, making random block decryption difficult.

The interdependency of the ciphertext blocks does present one problem, however. If any of the ciphertext gets corrupted, data entered after that point can't be retrieved because the key stream would be interrupted.

Since the DES algorithm is public information, the security of encrypted data depends solely on the strength of the encryption key. Effective key management goes hand in hand with data encryption. Users must maintain the secrecy of their keys while taking care not to forget them. Losing or forgetting a key would render the encrypted file useless.

Remember that an "unbreakable" code probably doesn't exist, but you can make your data so difficult to access that it is not worth the trouble for a thief to try. Of course the same considerations apply to both codes and passwords—they are meant to be kept secret and should not be put down on paper or disk where they can be read by unauthorized people.

LINE SECURITY

Before encryption, passwords, and user authorizations, comes line security. Obviously all of the other security measures wouldn't be necessary if you could keep unauthorized people off of the system in the first place.

One of the most vulnerable aspects of networked systems is the physical link used to connect the various systems. All electronic devices emit electromagnetic radiation, energy that moves through free air, which enables interception by diligent thieves with the proper equipment.

In addition, the wires used to carry signals among electronic systems emit radiation and sometimes can be tapped without physically violating the link. Proper detection equipment is usually neccessary to tell if the links were, indeed, broken and an unauthorized terminal or other device inserted in your network.

One way to avoid this type of security breach—and a method that will be automatic within a few years because of changing technology—is to replace copper wire with fiber optic cable. The only way to intercept information flowing over a fiber link is to physically break the cable or to interrupt the flow of information through one of the repeaters. Either of these security breaks is easier to detect than the external eavesdropping on an electrical cable.

Naturally if you are using conventional cable you can encase the wires in conduit, making it more difficult for anyone to get to the wire and reducing the possibility of electromagnetic emissions. Some building codes require conduits, especially for electric wires, but if you are worried about security you should consider conduits for all data wiring.

You can use nonremovable connectors where data cables attach to equipment or to each other. Look at the back of your TV set or cable company controller box. Chances are the main data cable, where it attaches to your equipment inside the house, is secured by a special connector that can't be removed without damaging the wire. Similar attachments can be used for network cables.

The TV cable companies have another security feature built into the system to prevent unscrupulous users from attaching more sets than they have paid for. The controller box—the channel selection device that sits between the cable and your TV—contains a small microprocessor and some code that enable it to communicate with a central computer at the local distribution office. If the connection is broken or anything else unusual occurs at the remote site, an error report can be generated in the office.

Many network management systems can be programmed to sample the quality of lines and the status of connections to remote devices such as gateways and bridges, providing the same kind of physical security and detection for your far-flung network.

HARDWARE SECURITY

There are several ways you can enhance the security of individual elements of a network system. A simple method that is frequently used with PCs and workstations is a lock and key. With the lock set you can't turn the system on or you can't use the keyboard.

In addition, you can use electronic keys, devices that attach to one of the computer's ports and send electronic signatures or codes into the system. The computer or node is programmed not to function unless this key is plugged into the proper port. When an authorized operator walks away from the system, the small electronic module is carried away too. Unless that unique electronic key sends the proper information to the terminal, PC, or host, you can't access the system.

Such electronic keys can take several forms. For example, you could program all nodes or workstations to accept authorized electronic keys, no matter where they are used in the system. This would allow anyone with proper authorization to carry their key to any network node and logon, as long as they plugged in the key.

On the other hand, you could put the lid on a little tighter by linking individual electronic keys to specific locations. That way users could only access the system from their authorized locations. If someone attempted to enter the system from an unauthorized location, even with the proper electronic key, an error condition would be detected and the proper people would be notified. ·

Some versions of the electronic key do not physically attach to the terminal; rather, they are the size of credit card computers that continually generate a series of pseudo-random numbers in concert with a program running on the host. Each user carries a card that is tied logically to their account information at one of the hosts on the network.

To access the system you have to enter the proper number displayed on your card at the precise moment you want to logon, and you have to enter the current user ID and password. You can even program such systems with emergency IDs or codes so that if a user is being forced to logon the system appears to work normally, but security personnel are notified and the source of the login is traced and reported.

For even tighter security, consider a biological identification system. There are several technologies, some of the most sophisticated used only by the federal government or the military. Ones you can buy off the shelf include fingerprint or handprint identifiers, eyeball scanners, and voice print devices.

You can erect a roadblock to your data at a dial-up link with any of these techniques, and in addition you can install a security modem. These intelligent modems can be set to accept the user ID and password, verify it, break the link, then dial the user back at a predefined telephone number. Like the electronic key tied to a specific node, this technique places a double level of security on each dial-up user. Not only must the user know the proper codes, but they also must be calling from their normal location.

Even if you don't implement a call back feature—possibly because remote users need access from a variety of locations—security modems isolate the caller from the system. Until the proper password and user ID are entered the modem does not even attach the caller to the network.

Security modems can also use encrypted transmissions that are linked to specific users (see the discussion of DES earlier in this chapter). That way, even if an unauthorized person secures a valid ID and password, unless they are using the proper modem programmed to use a specific encryption scheme, access is denied or the data is garbage.

Remember, too, that many host systems have a "back door" password put into place during set up or program development. Unless this back door is nailed shut when the system is put into general use, security can be compromised.

If you are installing a system be careful to verify that the back door has been closed. If you purchase a turnkey system from an outside vendor or consultant, it might be worthwhile to have another independent consultant check it out to make sure the back door is closed.

Of course, if a senior member of your MIS staff leaves the company, you should change any system-level passwords and operator codes.

ELECTRICAL SECURITY

Where data security is concerned don't overlook the need to protect your systems—and therefore your data—from physical damage.

A basic element to help ensure the security and well-being of all of your computer equipment is a surge protector, an electronic device usually embedded inside an extension cord, that helps isolate the electronic equipment from spikes and noise on the electrical wire. Figure 10.3 shows an example of a power protector. The quality of these units varies, however, so make

FIGURE 10.3 Power protection, such as with the Pulizzi PC 585 power distribution and control system, can put one more secure link in your system. [Reprinted with permission of Pulizzi Engineering, Inc.]

sure you purchase them from a reputable vendor and ask for engineering test data and testimonials. Be sure that everything in the system, including printers, plotters, modems, terminals, and monitors is protected.

For large and very critical installations you can install central power protection circuits that include uninterruptable power supplies, battery powered devices that provide enough current for an orderly shutdown in the event of a power outage. These UPS units also provide spike and overvoltage protection when they are in the line, even if regular AC power is not interrupted.

Don't overlook the other electrical line that enters your office and your computer—the telephone cable. Telephone lines are electrical conduits just like AC power lines and they are subject to the same static surges, even lightning. The line you are using doesn't have to take a direct hit to cause problems for sensitive equipment.

Consult your local telephone company about providing protection where the lines enter your building. You can also purchase small, inline, lightning protectors that attach at the device. Such modem line protectors are relatively inexpensive—$50 to $150— and they could save you from serious damage from lightning.

Remember that more than your modem is exposed, because the modem is attached to a host. Large voltage spikes can travel through the telephone line, into your modem, and out to the host. It is relatively rare, but it happens, so for enhanced data security investigate protection for everything hooked to the telephone line.

If you want to take surge protection a step further you can purchase an RS-232 grounding device that intercepts spikes and shunts them directly to ground. If you have such a unit between the host and any serial printers and between the host and the modems, you have an additional level of isolation in the event of telephone line or power line spikes to peripherals.

CHAPTER SUMMARY

Data security is not an insignificant problem, nor are there trivial solutions. Volumes have been written about it and some companies have complete staffs that work on nothing else. Although this chapter can't answer all of your security questions, it can serve as a starting point and a way of heightening your awareness of security issues.

At the simplest level there probably is nothing more important that you as a system manager or individual user can do than encourage and practice good password procedures. This is only one link in a complex and important chain, but it is one that can be strengthened—or weakened—at the individual user level.

While it is true that hackers and data pirates do exist, it is also true that the majority of information loss can be traced to a well-meaning or careless employee who is authorized to have access to the information. Security experts report that far more information is lost through carelessness or poor judgment than through outright theft.

Therefore, a successful security program must start at home, inside each company and department of the enterprise. Not only must individual users be taught the how and why of information security, they must be motivated to use it.

It is important to instill an overall awareness of security issues throughout your user community. Educate people on the value of computer data, show them how easy it can be to lose it, and motivate them to be protective of the information they control.

Serial Communications Reference

SERIAL STANDARDS
THE NONSTANDARD STANDARD
THE RS-232C CABLE
NONSTANDARD STANDARD CABLES
CENTRONICS STANDARD

In any host computer environment, the issue of serial communications is an important one. The majority of terminals connect to VAXs over serial lines, many printers use serial connections to a host or terminal server, and all modem and dial-up links involve serial communications.

This section discusses serial communications in general and identifies some of the problems you may encounter.

SERIAL STANDARDS

You assume when you buy light bulbs that they will screw into the sockets in the lamps in your home. You also assume that the lamp will have a plug that fits properly into the electrical outlet and that the outlet will provide voltage in the proper range. Finally, you feel confident that the bulb that carries a rating of 1600 lumens will glow at an expected, repeatable intensity equal to other bulbs with the same rating.

This is taken for granted because there is an established set of standards: hardware specifications for the bulb, socket, plug, and outlet; a "software" standard for voltage; and an agreed-upon rating for bulb brightness.

So it must be with computer telecommunications. Consider the following process:

You sit down at a computer keyboard to send a message across the country. The keyboard is familiar because the pressures of the marketplace have worked to make all such devices quite similar.

You start by typing "hello," assuming the recipient will understand this common language. If you speak French and you are communicating with someone else who speaks French, you would start by typing "bonjour." In a multilingual setting, you might start by typing "hello," the recipient might be able to quickly translate the message into "bonjour" and communication would continue.

This type of communication works because we have a standard alphabet. The computer understands the typed characters after it looks them up in a dictionary-like table and converts them to 0s and 1s in another standard—ASCII code.

Next, the computer sends those 0s and 1s to a modem that converts them to a standard modulated signal that can travel over a nationally standardized telephone system across the country. At the other end, another modem demodulates the signal and converts it back to 0s and 1s for the computer to look up in its table and translate back into characters.

The final step in our standardization journey calls for individuals to perceive the lines on a video screen, convert the outlines of characters, and then pick out the words and finally interpret the message.

THE NONSTANDARD STANDARD

The "spinal cord" for much of the computer-based communication is a serial cable. The recommended standard was developed by the Electronic Industries Association (EIA), a U.S. trade association. (You can obtain a copy of the standards by writing to: EIA Engineers' Department, Electronic Industries Association, 2001 Eye Street, N.W., Washington, D.C. 20006.)

It was created in 1969 to establish one official standard for making an interface between data terminal equipment (DTE) and data communications equipment (DCE) using serial digital data transmission. Today DTEs are more commonly referred to as computers and DCEs are generally called modems and printers.

The importance of the RS-232C standard is that it assigns specific types of signals to specific wires, or "pins" in a standard 25-pin cable. The "standard" defined the EIA position on electrical signal characteristics, the mechanical elements of the connection, and a functional assignment for interchange circuits. The RS-232C specification guarantees the integrity of signals transmitted over distances of up to 50 feet. In practice, data integrity will probably be alright at greater distances, and special cable and signal repeaters can be used to increase the distance significantly.

Basically the RS-232C standard means that any equipment that uses it can talk with any other piece of equipment that uses it. Unfortunately, however, everything is not neat and simple in the RS-232C standard world. For example, DCE and DTE interfaces aren't necessarily identical at both ends, all wires in the defined interface may or may not be connected straight through from one end to another, and finally, male and female versions of connectors sometimes differ from established standards.

In addition, with smaller footprint terminals and desktop machines, different vendors may use different connectors. Apple's implementation, for example, does not include the standard DB-25 plug for its original Macintosh series. The IBM PC serial port adapter terminates in a male connector while most other families of machines terminate their serial interfaces with a female outlet. Just to be more perverse, the IBM PC-AT terminates with a 9-pin D-shell that is similar to but not exactly like Apple's mini-plug.

Finally, taking a page from Alice in Wonderland, the EIA says that there are actually 13 standard but different implementations of the signal connections for an RS-232C interface. They've numbered them from A to M. But to confuse even that attempt at standardization, they added an "Interface Type Z" to stand for "anything else."

THE RS-232C CABLE

Actually, the 25 pins of the RS-232C cable are far more than are needed for most ordinary serial connections. For full duplex telecommunications between a terminal and a modem, for example, a maximum of 10 pins are probably used, as shown in Table A.1.

In fact, systems in the VAX environment that use logical flow control (communication that tells each device the state of the connected device) instead of electrical flow control, only three or four wires may be used for some links.

Here's a step-by-step sequence of a computer-to-modem-to-modem-to-computer connection using an RS-232C interface and cable.

1. The computer (DTE) raises the voltage on pin 20, signalling to the modem (DCE) that the computer is ready

TABLE A.1. Telecommunications Sample

DTE (Computer)		DCE (Modem)	The message
1	Frame ground	1	Common "earth" ground
2	Transmit data	2	Data being sent
3	Receive data	3	Data being received
4	Request to send	4	"May I send?"
5	Clear to send	5	"Yes, you may."
6	Data set ready	6	"The modem is ready."
7	Signal ground	7	Common signal wire
8	Data carrier detect	8	"The link is okay."
20	Data ready terminal	20	"The terminal is ready."
22	Ring indicator	22	"The phone is ringing."

to communicate. The signal is called "data terminal ready."

2. If a dial-up link is used, the telephone number is dialed either manually by the user or by the modem under direction of software.

3. The remote or "answer" modem at the other end of the phone line detects the incoming ring signal and sends an answer back in the form of a carrier signal.

4. The dialing or "originate" modem detects the carrier tone and then raises the voltage on two wires going back to the computer: the "data set ready" signal on pin 6 and the "data carrier detect" on line 8. (The official Bell term for modem is "data set.")

5. The computer asks permission to send information by raising the voltage on pin 4, "request to send" (RTS).

6. The modem responds to the RTS query with a "clear to send" (CTS) signal on pin 5.

7. Data begins to flow from the computer to the modem, which converts it from digital 0s and 1s to an analog warble. Data is sent out on line 2, entering the receiving computer on pin 3. Both computers continually monitor lines 4, 6, 8, and 20 to determine that communication is possible. This is the hardware handshaking.

NONSTANDARD STANDARD CABLES

In the simplest scheme, a computer could be connected to a modem with just three wires: the signal ground on pin 7, the transmitted data on pin 2, and the received data incoming on pin 3. In such an arrangement, of course, there is no handshaking between systems to arrange for timing and error checking, and it would probably be best not to use such a cable to connect one or more "smart" modems—modems with timing, error checking, and other functions built in—since they could become confused by the unorthodox wiring scheme.

In many short-distance applications, the easiest way to connect two computers is through a direct link between their serial ports, using a special RS-232C cable, a null modem.

This cable connects the transmit wire (pin 2) of computer A to the receive wire (pin 3) of computer B, and vice versa. Such a cable is also called a crossover cable or modem eliminator.

Another type of cable can be used to connect two computers of unequal intelligence. This wiring scheme fools a transmitting computer into thinking it has CTS when it asks RTS. It also assures the more demanding computer that the data set is ready (DSR) and that a carrier signal has been detected (CD). Such jumpered cables are frequently used when logical handshaking instead of hardware handshaking will be used.

```
Ground   7   —-  7
DTR     20   —|
DSR      6   ←|
DCD      8   ←|
RTS      4   —|
CTS      5   ←|
TxD      2   —-  2
RxD      3   —-  3
```

Table A.2 shows the full RS-232C wiring specification standard.

Figure A.1 shows the RS-232 interface.

TABLE A.2. The RS-232C Standard

Pin	Name of Signal	Direction
1	Earth ground	
2	Transmitted data	To DCE
3	Received data	To DTE
4	Request to send	To DCE
5	Clear to send	To DTE
6	Data set ready	To DTE
7	Logic ground	
8	Carrier detect	To DTE
9	Reserved*(+ transmit current loop return 20 ma)	
10	Reserved	
11	Reserved*(− transmit current loop data 20 ma)	
12	Secondary carrier detect	To DTE
13	Secondary clear to send	To DTE
14	Secondary transmitted data	To DCE
15	Transmit clock	To DTE
16	Secondary received data	To DTE
17	Receiver clock	To DTE
18	Reserved*(+ receive current loop data 20 ma)	
19	Secondary request to send	To DCE
20	Data terminal ready	To DCE
21	Signal quality detect	To DTE
22	Ring detect	To DTE
23	Data rate select	To DCE
24	Transmit clock	To DCE
25	Reserved*(− receive current loop return 20 ma)	

*Pins 9, 11, 18, and 25 are IBM implementation of current loop

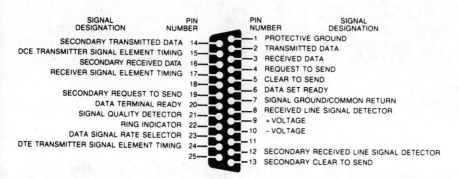

FIGURE A.1 Many RS-232 cables attach with a DB-25 connector. [Reprinted with permission of Black Box Corporation]

CENTRONICS STANDARD

The other major standard for communications is parallel transmission, in which the seven or eight bits of the signal moved down seven or eight parallel wires, with each computer word arriving at the same moment.

The Centronics standard, named after the printer company that popularized it, is the principal parallel standard. IEEE-488 is another parallel standard used in some computers. IEEE-488 signals require conversion before they can be used with Centronics devices.

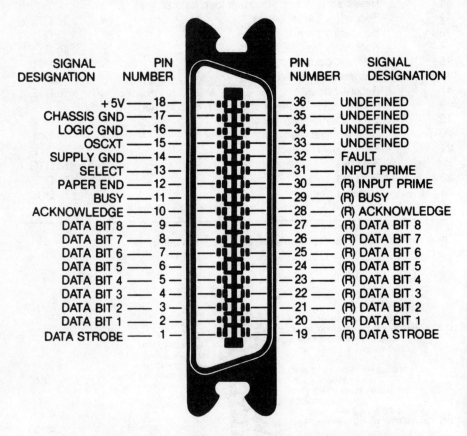

SIGNAL DESIGNATION	PIN NUMBER		PIN NUMBER	SIGNAL DESIGNATION
+5V	18		36	UNDEFINED
CHASSIS GND	17		35	UNDEFINED
LOGIC GND	16		34	UNDEFINED
OSCXT	15		33	UNDEFINED
SUPPLY GND	14		32	FAULT
SELECT	13		31	INPUT PRIME
PAPER END	12		30	(R) INPUT PRIME
BUSY	11		29	(R) BUSY
ACKNOWLEDGE	10		28	(R) ACKNOWLEDGE
DATA BIT 8	9		27	(R) DATA BIT 8
DATA BIT 7	8		26	(R) DATA BIT 7
DATA BIT 6	7		25	(R) DATA BIT 6
DATA BIT 5	6		24	(R) DATA BIT 5
DATA BIT 4	5		23	(R) DATA BIT 4
DATA BIT 3	4		22	(R) DATA BIT 3
DATA BIT 2	3		21	(R) DATA BIT 2
DATA BIT 1	2		20	(R) DATA BIT 1
DATA STROBE	1		19	(R) DATA STROBE

(R) INDICATES SIGNAL GROUND RETURN

FIGURE A.2 The Centronics 36-pin connector. [Reprinted with permission of Black Box Corporation]

TABLE A.3. Centronics Pins and Signal Descriptions.

Signal Pin No.	Return Pin No.	Signal	Direction (with ref. to printer)	Description
1	19	STROBE	In	STROBE pulse (negative going) enables reading data.
2	20	DATA 1	In	1st to 8th bits of parallel data.
3	21	DATA 2	In	Each signal is at "HIGH" level when data is logical
4	22	DATA 3	In	"1" and "LOW" when logical "0"
5	23	DATA 4	In	
6	24	DATA 5	In	
7	25	DATA 6	In	
8	26	DATA 7	In	
9	27	DATA 8	In	
10	28	ACKNLG	Out	"LOW" indicates that data has been received and that the printer is ready to accept other data.
11	29	BUSY	Out	"HIGH" indicates that the printer cannot receive data.

Note: Pins 12, 13, 14, 15, 18, 31, 32, 34, 35, and 36 vary in function depending upon application; they are commonly used for printer auxiliary controls, and error handling and indication.

Pins 16 and 17 are commonly used for logic ground and chassis ground, respectively.

Reprinted with permission of Black Box Corporation.

The 36-pin Centronics standard is set up to carry the eight bits of a computer word along eight parallel lines so that each byte arrives at its destination at the same instant (see Figure A.2).

Holding the plug facing you with the wider face to the right, the pins are numbered from 1 at left bottom up the left side to 18; and from 19 at the right bottom up the right side to 36 (see Table A.3).

Modem Reference

Appendix B is provided to help you understand some of the finer points of modem operation and selection, including modem standards.

MODEM STANDARDS

In theory, any type of modulation that is compatible with and does not damage the public telephone or common carrier network could be used to transmit information from point to point. In the early days of telecommunications, there were several "standards" in use.

Racal-Vadic, in the early 1970s, was the first American firm to sell a 1200-baud modem, using what the company called the "3400 protocol." A few years later, Bell Labs entered the marketplace with a 1200-baud device based on what it called the 212A standard. Bell's system won out simply because of the company's size. There are still Racal-Vadic modems in use, but they either now include the 212A standard or they can only be used to communicate with other 3400-protocol devices.

The Bell standards are divided into 100 and 200 series. The Bell 100 series operates at speeds up to 300 baud and can transmit and receive simultaneously (full-duplex). Standards 113A and 113B also run at 300 baud, but only in half-duplex mode.

The Bell 200 series encompasses 1200 baud communication. Bell standard 202 is 1200 baud, but only half-duplex. Bell standard 212A is 1200 baud, full-duplex, and also capable of downshifting to slower rates.

THE INTERNATIONAL ARENA

The international community relies primarily upon "recommendations" from the Comite Consultatif International Telegraphique et Telephonique (CCITT), a committee of the United Nations International Telecommunications Union (ITU). That agency comprises representatives from more than 80 countries as well as delegations from several major private telecommunications agencies, including AT&T, Western Union, RCA Global Communications Corp., and Nippon Telephone and Telegraphic Public Co.

All CCITT recommendations for small computers are assigned a V or X prefix. The V series of standards are for data communication over the existing switched telephone network, while the X code denotes standards for data communication networks and other communications that do not use switched phone lines. Revisions or alternate recommendations for the same standard are indicated by "bis" (second) or "ter" (third), as in the X.25 bis standard for networking. (In addition to modem standards, the CCITT has recommendations V.24 and V.28 that generally parallel the RS-232C interface standard from the EIA.)

The Bell 212A standard is likely to be around a long time because of its huge installed base. The CCITT has come up with a corresponding—but incompatible—standard called V.22.

CCITT has a 300-baud standard called V.21 that is not compatible with Bell 103. The V.22 standard is a near equivalent to Bell 212A, but not fully compatible with it. (There is also a V.23 standard which is used in European videotext with an unusual bidirectional speed limit: 1200 baud for incoming graphics and information and 75 baud for outgoing commands from terminals.)

Before you despair of ever finding a way to link your American and European offices, let's differentiate direct dial-up from public telecommunications networks. To communicate directly at 1200 baud, you will either have to have Bell 212A devices at both ends (illegally at the European side) or V.22 devices at both ends.

One solution is to use one of the international networks, such as Tymnet, Telenet, or Euronet, that provide their own protocol converters. All the user needs is a modem that is compatible from the micro to the node and from the node to the micro.

BUYING A MODEM

Congratulations! You've made the decision to connect your workstation with the VAX via a modem. That was simple, wasn't it?

Not exactly. There are modems and there are modems. Here are some of the decisions you still must make:

- 300, 1200, 2400, or 9600 baud?
- Error correcting? Using which protocol?
- Direct-connect or acoustic coupled?
- Internal or external?
- Smart or dumb?
- Hayes compatible?

MODEM SPECIFICATIONS

In many ways, modems have become commodities. There is not a great deal of difference in performance between models with similar features from different manufacturers. Decide first on the capabilities you need and then look at the specification sheets for modems that offer those features. You'll also find regular modem reviews in computer magazines.

How much speed do you need in a modem? Part of the answer lies in defining how fast is fast. Let's start by striking the 300-baud modem off your list: the price differential between a 300-baud and a 1200-baud modem—once several hundred dollars—is now so slight as to be inconsequential. And any user would find 300-baud communication to be the electronic equivalent of a job watching cement dry. The only reason to use 300-baud modems these days is if the quality of your dial-up telephone service is so poor that nothing faster will work.

Remember, too, that almost all 1200-baud modems can be instructed to operate at the slower 300-baud speed; 2400-baud models can be downshifted to 1200 or 300 baud. This will allow you some flexibility for communicating with other users. And because 300-baud devices are less demanding of a perfect phone connection, you may be able to use the slower speed as a backup.

The same argument holds for 2400-baud modems. By shopping carefully you can purchase a 2400-baud device for around $100, or you can drop down to 1200 baud and pay only $60 or so. We have seen a few 2400-baud "specials" offered in discount magazines for around $75. When you consider that a modem should last three to five years, the price differential is not significant. In fact, if you use online services that charge by the minute, you will pay for the faster modem in online charge savings fairly quickly.

One measure of modem design quality is the carrier-detect threshold. This is a measure of the strength of signal required by the modem for communications. Indicated in decibels, the greater the negative dB value the better the modem is at finding a weak carrier signal on a noisy telephone line. A threshold of −45 dB or lower is a good indication.

A MEASURE OF SPEED

You can approximate the transmission time of a document with a simple mathematical progression. First, determine the size of the file in bytes.

Let's say the file you've selected is 30,720 bytes long. Each byte represents a character. Simply divide the number of bytes by the character-per-second (cps) speed of your modem. Add about one-third more time to account for framing bits and other control characters. The result will be the approximate transmission time, in seconds, for the file. In this instance, we divide 30,720 by 120 cps to yield a result of 256 seconds. Multiply that figure times 1.3 for framing bits to yield an approximate transmission time of 333 seconds, or 5 minutes and 33 seconds. If we were to send this file with a 300-baud modem, it would take about 22 minutes and 12 seconds to transmit.

You can also look at the number of bytes in a file and come up with an approximation of the number of words contained within it. In English-language text, the average length of a word is 5.5 characters. Add another "character" to represent spaces and you have a word length of 6.5 units. Divide the number of bytes in a simple ASCII text file by 6.5 and you will obtain a rough word count for the file.

It is not quite so simple to apply this method to a file created in a special format for a word processor—the file may contain a very high percentage of extra characters for overhead, including formatting and indexing codes.

It is also possible to purchase a word-counting utility that will go into the file and come up with a number. Most of these programs work by counting the number of spaces between sets of characters and presenting that result as the number of words in the file. Such utilities are generally accurate to within about 10 percent of the actual number of words.

Let's say you know the number of words in a file. This chart shows transmission times for typical documents.

Words in document	300 baud	1200 baud	2400 baud
1000	3:20	0:50	0:25
3000	10:00	2:30	1:15
5000	16:40	4:10	2:05
10000	33:20	8:20	4:10

Transmission times in this chart assume near-perfect line conditions. Remember that a 1200-baud modem that is forced to send every block of data four times, because of a poor telephone connection, is ultimately no faster than a 300-baud modem with an acceptable connection.

GOING FOR A SHORT HAUL

All modems aren't used for dial-up communications. One type of modem, called a "short-haul" modem or "line driver," is designed to provide high-speed connections over short distances. Priced in the midrange, line drivers use standard computer cable, special twisted-pair wire circuits, or dedicated telephone circuits. They are not designed for use with dial-up phone circuits. A typical model might work at speeds of up to 19,200 baud for up to a mile, 9600 baud for a six-mile range, and 2400 baud for ten-mile transmissions. Units are available to carry asynchronous as well as synchronous communication, and some devices include multiplexing circuitry, allowing transmission of several piggy-backed signals on the same line.

INTELLIGENT MODEMS

A "smart" modem is a modem with its own microprocessor and a small amount of memory that is capable of receiving instructions directly from the user or indirectly from a communications program.

Some standard features of intelligent modems include the following:

Auto dialing. Uses software or keyboard to dial phone numbers automatically, usually presenting a choice between pulse (a simulation of a rotary dialing phone) or tone (electronic equivalence to the Bell Touch-Tone system).

Auto answer. Allows the modem to detect incoming calls and function without operator involvement for bulletin board or other systems. Some modems can also operate in the background without affecting other tasks performed by the computer.

Programmable parameters. Parameters such as baud rate, protocols, and other features can be selected through direct command by the user or through instructions passed along by communications software.

Autobaud. Provides capability to determine the baud rate of an incoming signal and automatically adjust to match it. This is a particularly important feature for remote systems.

Originate/answer selection. A modem must be set up as either the originator or the answerer of a phone call so that the devices can send and receive signals at the proper frequencies. Some modems have an originate/answer switch, while some programmable modems can detect which mode it must operate in and set themselves.

Other useful features available in modems include the following:

Voice and data transmission. The ability to switch back and forth between data and voice transmission with the aid of hardware or software switches. This is very valuable for giving quick instructions to the party at the other end. You will require, of course, a telephone handset plugged into the system at some point.

Positive tone detection. A feature that allows a smart modem to listen into the line for secondary dial tones such as those required by PBX systems in offices or by some long-distance services. For example, if you must dial 9 and wait for a second dial tone to get an outside line, a smart modem can be instructed to wait for a specified period of time or to wait to detect a second carrier tone.

Error and indicator lights. A visual indication of the status of the modem. If you are using an internal modem, some devices will send messages to be displayed on the screen.

Volume control and speaker shutoff. Most autodialing modems will include a small speaker to allow the user to listen in for the dial tone, dialing pulses or tones, rings, and carrier signal as an aural check on the progress of the call. Valuable features to accompany the speaker are a volume control and an automatic shutoff of the speaker once a connection is made.

Test mode. Some devices include a self-diagnosis program that checks out the system when it is turned on, and others will even report on the quality of the phone line when first activated.

THE HAYES STANDARD

Hayes Microcomputer Products was an early success in the modem business and remains an important force in the industry. Its initial modems were among the first with a built-in microprocessor capable of responding to instructions from the host computer—to change parameters or protocols and to dial numbers, among other tasks. Though many other companies have since introduced modems with equal or enhanced features, the Hayes model became the unofficial standard. Many software packages were written to take advantage of the Hayes instruction set, and you will find many unrelated modem manufacturers advertising their devices as "Hayes-compatible."

Why might it be advantageous to use a modem with a particular command set? The answer is mostly related to the communications software package you will use with the hardware. The use of a standard should allow the software to automate such procedures as dialing, connecting, responding with passwords and requests for specific services, and the like. Almost all communications software is designed for a Hayes or Hayes-compatible modem. Check for support of your particular piece of hardware before making a purchase.

There are two parts to the unofficial Hayes standard: the panel of indicator lights on the external model, and the set of "attention" codes and instructions for the microprocessor. (On a modem mounted internally, it is not possible to read the indicator lights directly, although some units will echo status messages to the screen.)

THE HAYES INDICATOR LIGHTS

From right to left on a Hayes Smartmodem 1200 model, the indicator lights are as follows:

MR *Modem ready*. Remains lit while power to the modem is on.

TR *Terminal ready*. Shows that a signal has been sent to the Smartmodem, and that the data terminal is ready to receive or send data or to accept commands from the terminal. Depending upon selection of a configuration switch setting, TR will be illuminated whenever power to the modem is on, or only when power is on and the power to the computer or terminal is on. The second setting can only be used if the computer or terminal supports the RS-232C data terminal ready signal (pin 20).

SD *Send data*. Lights up when data or commands are sent from the serial port to the modem. In other words, SD is an indicator of incoming signals to the modem from the locally attached computer or terminal.

RD *Receive data*. An indication that data is being sent from the modem to its controlling computer. In full duplex mode,

RD will also light as the modem echoes back data sent by the controlling computer. RD will also illuminate when the modem sends result codes to the local computer, indicating the presence of a carrier or the discontinuance of a link.

OH *Off hook.* Lights up when the modem is using the telephone line.

CD *Carrier detect.* Indicates when the modem has detected a carrier signal from a remote modem.

AA *Auto-answer.* If the modem has been placed in the automatic answering mode, either by the setting of a hardware switch or the transmission of a software code, this light will be illuminated. When the phone rings, the AA light will go off during each ring, and the line will be answered after a specified number of rings.

HS *High speed.* Lights up to indicate that the modem is set at its highest speed, in the case of the Smartmodem 1200, at 1200 baud.

AT COMMANDS

The software command structure of the Hayes standard is based around the "AT" (attention) instruction and the "S" registers of the modem. Most commands must begin with the AT prefix— this is used by the modem both as an indicator of an upcoming instruction and as a benchmark for automatic settings. The modem looks at the incoming "A" to determine the speed of transmission of the computer or terminal; the "T" gives enough information for word length and parity to be determined.

Depending upon how you use your modem and the type of communications software you employ, you may never input an AT command directly or you may constantly be giving the modem direct instructions. Either way, it's worthwhile to have some understanding of the nature of the communication between the computer and modem.

Here are a few of the AT commands as implemented on the Smartmodem 1200:

Dialing Commands

D   *Dial*. Puts the modem in originate mode to dial a number.

,   *Pause*. Makes the modem wait for a second dial tone before continuing to dial a number. Used with PBX systems to get an outside line, or with secondary long-distance services like MCI, Sprint, and SBS.

T   *Touch-tone dialing*. Uses Bell standard DTMF tones.

P   *Pulse dialing*. Mimics a rotary-dial phone in dialing.

R   *Reverse mode*. Allows the modem to dial an originate-only modem.

A/   *Repeats the last command*. Often used to re-dial a phone number.

;   Puts the modem back in the *command state* after dialing.

For example, the command

```
ATDT 5551212
```

would set the modem on Touch-tone dialing and call the phone number. You would hear the dial tone and then the electronic tones as the call is placed.
The command

```
ATDP 12125551212
```

adds an access code, an area code, and the instruction to dial using pulses instead of Touch-tone signals. You can place spaces or dashes in the phone number to help visualize the number, as in this example:

```
ATDP 1-212 555-1212
```

Dialing out with a PBX system, you would add one or more commas to have the modem pause and wait for secondary dial tones. You can also change from pulse to Touch-tone if, for example, the PBX is an old-style pulse or rotary dial system while the phone exchange can accept tones. Here is an example:

ATDP 9,T1518 555-1212

HAYES MODEM REGISTERS

The S registers of the Hayes and Hayes-like modems allow settings for a number of parameters. Timing for several modem events are as follows:

S0 Sets the number of rings before the Smartmodem will answer a call. A value of 0 will instruct the modem not to answer the phone. A value from 1 through 255 indicates ring numbers for auto-answering.

S6 Sets length of time the Smartmodem will wait for a dial tone before dialing the first digit of a phone number. Default value is 2 seconds.

S7 Sets length of time the modem will wait for a carrier signal after conclusion of dialing. Default value is 30 seconds.

S8 Sets length of pause for each comma in command. Default value is 2 seconds.

S9 Sets duration of time the Smartmodem will listen to a carrier signal before recognition. Default value is 600 milliseconds.

S10 Sets time between loss of carrier signal and disconnection of line. Default value is 700 milliseconds.

S11 Sets duration and spacing of Touch-tone dialing tones. Default value is 70 milliseconds.

Commands sent to the S-register follow the format AT SX = X. For example, if your PBX system is particularly slow and you need to instruct the modem to wait longer for a dial tone for an outside line, the following command could be used:

```
AT S6 = 5
```

The modem will echo back a response of "OK" to the monitor if the command has been successfully acted upon.

MULTIPLEXERS

Multiplexers are devices that accept two or more lines of data from computers and then transmit them at high-speed to a central computer. They are typically used with terminals or remote computers in synchronous or asynchronous communication over dedicated phone lines. In a typical setup, RS-232C output cables from terminals or computers are plugged into a line multiplexer and the output of that device is plugged into a standard modem. The output of the modem enters the phone line. At the other end, the phone line goes into the modem and the output of the modem goes into another multiplexer that splits the signal into outputs for the central computer.

Many multiplex units include automatic adjustments to match exchange rates with modems, and also feature error correction circuitry. The principal advantages of using multiplex units are simplicity of connection and cost savings compared to expensive dedicated lines and individual modems.

CONCENTRATORS

A variant of the multiplexer is a device called a concentrator. Concentrators combine data from many slow terminals and transmit the recombined data stream to the host at a very high speed, reducing the need for leased lines. Typically, it has more than two lines connected.

Glossary

20mA: Host port connector: A port on the back of a VT terminal used to connect the device to a nearby host computer using a 20 milliamp connection.

8088: The Intel microprocessor that is the brain of the PC and most PC-compatible machines. Processes 16-bit words internally, but deals with the computer through an 8-bit bus.

68020: A high-speed, 16-bit microprocessor that is common in workstations and network processors. The 68020 is being superseded in new applications by the 68030 processor.

80188: A true 16-bit version of the Intel 8088 chip. Used in some PC compatible machines.

80286: A high-speed, true 16-bit member of the Intel 8088 family. Used as the brain of the PC-AT.

80287: The 16-bit equivalent of the 8087 Math Coprocessor. Available for use with the 80286 chip in the PC-AT.

A: Ampere. A measurement of the strength of a current of electricity.

AC: Alternating current. An electrical flow that reverses its direction at regular intervals.

Access control: The process of validating a connection, login, or file access request to see if the action is permitted under the instructions set by the system manager. Access control is usually implemented through the use of passwords.

Access line: The direct connection from the telephone equipment at your premises to the nearest telephone office. Also called a local loop.

Access protocol: The scheme employed by a network to avoid data collisions, such as carrier sense multiple access. Also called media access control.

Access time: The amount of time required to store or retrieve information. Memory chip speeds are typically measured in nanoseconds; disk speeds are measured in microseconds.

Account: The heart of the system's accounting and library functions. Every user of the system, including many of the parts of the system itself, has an account assigned by the system manager. The computer keeps track of the privileges assigned to each account as well as the physical location of the files created by or sent to each account.

Accumulator: A register in a microprocessor that gathers and stores the result of an operation.

ACK: A control character that is part of a telecommunications handshaking protocol, transmitted by a receiver to acknowledge that a character or block of characters has been received.

Acoustic coupler: A form of modem in which the digital signals of the computer are converted into audio tones and transmitted by a speaker to a telephone handset. At the receiving end, a microphone picks up incoming audio tones and converts them to digital signals. Compare to direct-connect modem.

Active position: The location on the screen, indicated by the cursor, where the next typed character will appear.

Active window: The frontmost window displayed on a screen.

Address: A number used by the operating system to identify the location of information in storage. Can be regarded as virtual address or physical address. In many computers, address locations are identified in terms of a starting address for a block of memory and an offset address identifying how far into that block a particular bit of data is located.

Address bus: One or more conductors used to carry the binary-encoded address from the microprocessor through the rest of the system.

Algorithm: A formula or logical method used to solve a problem or accomplish a task. Conversion of binary data to ASCII characters requires an algorithm, for example. The efficiency of an algorithm is an unseen contributor to the speed of a modem, computer, or communications process.

Alias: A different name for the same entity, allowing use of shorter or more familiar names for complex commands, files, or specifications.

Allocate a device: The user can reserve a device for exclusive use. Such an action can only be made when the device is not allocated by another process.

Alphanumeric character: An alphabetic letter in upper- or lower-case, any decimal digit, plus the dollar sign and the underscore.

Analog: The representation of numerical quantities by the measurement of continuous physical variables. For example, the rise and fall of a wave-like signal is an analog signal, becoming an analogy of the effect being measured— the stronger the signal the higher the wave. In telephone communication, the signal carries information by continuously varying the electrical frequency wave to match the sound frequencies and volume of the input signal. In an automobile, the standard speedometer registers on an analog scale, with greater speed indicated by greater deflection of the needle. The other form of data manipulated by a computer is digital and based on purely numerical codes.

ANSI: American National Standards Institute. The principal American standards development organization and representative of the U.S. to the International Standards Organization (ISO).

ANSI characters: A set of characters established as a standard by the American National Standards Institute. Two types of ANSI sets are graphic and control characters. See graphic characters, and see control characters.

APL: Abbreviation of a programming language, an advanced language that makes heavy use of symbols instead of words for communication with the computer. Requires hardware or software enhancements to allow display of its non-ASCII character set on many computers.

APPC: Advanced program-to-program communications. An IBM protocol that is similar to the OSI session layer. It is responsible for setting the conditions to allow multiple application programs to send data across a network.

Application layer: The topmost layer of the OSI model, responsible for defining the manner in which application programs work with the operating system.

Application program: A set of computer instructions intended to perform a specific task, such as a spreadsheet, word processor, or database program.

Arbitration: In a computer, the management by a piece of hardware or software of multiple requests for the same channel at the same time. For example, on a network, there must be a form of arbitration to handle the possibility that two stations will seek to transmit at the same time. The arbitration can be random or it can be based on a logical assessment of priorities.

Architecture: The hardware design of a computer or peripheral that determines its compatibility with other such devices.

Archiving: The act of backing up a file to a different disk for the purpose of safeguarding the data against loss.

ARCnet: Attached resources computing network. A token-passing bus network.

ARQ: Automatic request for repetition. Part of a handshaking protocol. Sent by the receiving computer to request retransmission of a signal when an error has been detected.

ASCII: Abbreviation for American Standard Code for Information Interchange, a standard that defines the coding for letters, numbers, and symbols manipulated by computers, printers, or plotters. Pronounced "as-key."

ASCII characters: The American Standard Code for Information Interchange, a set of 8-bit binary numbers used to represent the alphabet and other symbols used by the computer in many communications, display, and printing applications.

ASIC: Application-specific integrated circuit. A microchip designed and fabricated for a specific purpose. Also called a "custom chip."

Assembly language: A programming language that directly speaks to the computer. The VAX uses a language referred to as VAX MACRO.

Assign a channel: The creation of a software link between a user process and a device unit to allow communication with a device.

Asynchronous: The transmission of information over a single wire, one bit at a time. Each character is framed by a start bit and one or more stop bits, and thus the transmission of information is not dependent upon precise timing between receiver and transmitter. Compare with synchronous communication.

Attached processor: A secondary processor in certain types of VAX systems.

Attenuation: The reduction or loss of signal strength, measured in decibels (dBs) or in decibels-per-unit-length (kilometer or mile). Virtually all electrical conductors suffer from attenuation. At some point a signal cannot be sent any further without amplification or retransmission. The opposite of attenuation is gain.

Auditing: A notation by the system that a particular event has taken place.

Authentication: The establishment of the identity and privileges of users signing on to a computer.

Auto print mode: A printing mode that sends the currently displayed line to a printer each time the on-screen cursor moves down a line because of a linefeed, form feed, vertical tab code, or auto wrap situation. Auto print is selectable from within the print menu of the set-up series of menus. All printing functions, including print screen, can be initiated from the keyboard while in this mode. See printing modes for other conditions.

Auto-answer: The capability of a modem to automatically establish a connection when a phone "rings" with an incoming call. Usually coupled with auto-dial abilities allowing dialing of phone numbers from a computer file or keyboard.

Auto-dial: The ability of a modem or associated software to place a telephone call for voice or data communication.

Autorepeat: A feature of a terminal that allows most keys to send their character repeatedly when the key is held down. The autorepeat feature can be turned on or off using the keyboard set-up screen of VT220 and VT300 terminals.

Auxiliary keyboard: Same as numeric keyboard.

Background: A procedure run during idle moments by a processor or server, allowing another procedure to take precedence in the foreground. For example, a printing job could be undertaken while the computer is mostly occupied with another text editing procedure.

Backup copy: A copy of a program made for storage and used only in case of problems with an original.

Backup file: A copy of the most recently edited version of a file, kept in case the current version is somehow destroyed or altered inappropriately. Some word processors automatically create a backup file anytime an existing file is edited. A truly cautious user will make backup files of irreplaceable documents on separate disks that will be stored in a different place from data files in daily use. As a verb, to backup means to create a protective file. The act of recovering a backed-up file is to restore.

Bandwidth: The frequency range of a channel—the difference between the highest and lowest frequencies of a transmission signal. Usually measured in kilohertz or megahertz. The wider the bandwidth, the greater the theoretical capacity of the channel.

Basic-group signal: In an analog telephone network, a signal that combines 12 voiceband channels within a bandwidth of 60 to 108 kilohertz.

Basic rate interface: See BRI.

Batch processing: A system under which a computer accepts and stores for execution all of the commands of a particular process or program and then executes them as a group. Contrast to real-time processing.

Baudot code: The five-bit code used in Telex systems.

Baud rate: The speed at which a terminal or modem communicates with the host system, printer, or other device. The actual measurement is of the number of discrete signal changes per second. At slower speeds, each signal change may represent a single bit, and therefore the baud rate would be the same as the number of bits per second. At higher-speed communication, one change in signal can represent two or more bits. For successful serial communication, the baud rate of computer and peripheral must be the same. The name is derived from J.M.E. Baudot (1845–1903), a French telegraphy pioneer.

Binary machine code: The internal language of the computer, stored and executed on the basis of a binary (two-character, 0 and 1) code. Programmers use languages, compiler, and the VAX macro assembler to generate the binary code for the computer.

Bell 103:   The AT&T standard for asynchronous telecommunication at speeds up to 300 baud.

Bell 201:   The AT&T standard for asynchronous telecommunication at speeds up to 2400 bits-per-second.

Bell 202:   The AT&T standard for asynchronous telecommunication at speeds up to 1800 bits-per-second. Requires a four-wire line for full-duplex transmission.

Bell 208:   The AT&T standard for synchronous telecommunication at speeds up to 4800 bits-per-second.

Bell 209:   The AT&T standard for synchronous telecommunication at speeds up to 9600 bits-per-second.

Bell 212:   The AT&T standard for full-duplex asynchronous or synchronous transmission at speeds up to 1200 bits-per-second on dial-up phone lines.

Binary synchronous communications (BSC):   An IBM protocol using a standardized set of control characters and protocols for the synchronous exchange of information. The transmitter and receiver beat to the same synchronizing control characters as they communicate. See synchronous transmission.

Bisynchronous: See binary synchronous communications.

Bit: The basic unit of information recognized by a computer. Derived from the phrase "binary digit." A bit can have only one of two values: off or on (also recognized as 0 or 1).

Bit map: A video screen is made up of a grid divided into units called pixels (picture elements). Each pixel is controlled by bits that set intensity and color. An entire screenful of such information is referred to as a bit map. Bit map graphics can also be used to produce an image using a dot matrix printer.

Block graphics: Pictures produced by a monitor or printer using ASCII characters such as lines, boxes, slashes, and parts of curves.

Boot: To bootstrap, or bring a program or machine to a desired state by its own action.

Boot name: The name of the device used to boot software.

BPS: Bits per second. The rate at which data moves. See also baud rate.

Break: In telecommunications, the condition that results when a device maintains a "space" state over a transmission line for a period of at least one frame.

Break key: A key that is recognized by some programs and operating system states as meaning a halt to a particular process or program or a disconnect. The Break key sends different commands in its ordinary, shifted, and Ctrl combinations.

Breakout box: A device for troubleshooting or temporary fixes for telecommunications wiring that allow enabling or disabling, jumpering, or merging of signals.

BRI: basic rate interface. Within ISDN, a format consisting of two bearer (B) channels operating at 64 kilobits-per-second and one signaling (D) channel operating at 16 kilobits-per-second.

Bridges: Devices which connect between networks, allowing nodes on either network to work with nodes on the other. A standard bridge does not amplify signals or control their flow. See also gateways.

Broadcast addressing: A means of sending a message to all nodes of a system.

Broadcast circuit: A circuit to which multiple nodes are connected and across which a message can be sent to multiple receivers.

Buffer: A storage place for data that compensates for differences in speed of data flow between two devices. A printer or plotter typically operates on instructions at a rate much slower than a computer can send it, and a buffer can be used to accept and store instructions. Also, some word processors allow placement of a block of copy into a buffer within the computer's RAM. This copy can later be recalled and inserted elsewhere in the file. Programs that have an "Undelete" function will place the most recent character manipulation into a buffer to allow resetting.

Buffered repeaters: Amplifiers that are not electrically continuous to the cable. These devices can control the flow of signals by issuing "start" and "stop" commands to avoid collisions. See also repeaters.

Bulletin board: A community service for posting or reading of messages, files, and programs.

Bus: A network design in which a signal passes through all nodes enroute to the designated recipient. A bus has a certain topology that determines the pathways in which data moves to all of the stations, or nodes, on the network. Each point on the network must be able to recognize those messages addressed to it, and there must be a means of arbitration by the system so that multiple points on the network do not attempt to send data at the same instant.

Bus: On a microcomputer, the system bus carries the electrical connections between the microprocessor and its memory, controllers, and peripherals. The bus is generally part of the backplane or mother board and actually consists of an address bus (g), a data bus, power supply lines, and other control lines.

Byte: Eight contiguous bits, used by the computer to store numbers or characters. Bits are numbered from 0 to 7, going from right to left. Bit 7 is the "sign bit," indicating a positive or negative integer. Bits are counted in binary, or two's complement mathematics, and thus a 7-bit byte can be in the range from $+128$ to -128. Without the sign bit, the number can range from 0 to 255 in decimal counting.

C: A programming language used on a wide range of microcomputers and highly regarded because of the relative ease with which programs can be translated from one system to another.

Cache: A means to speed user access to data by setting aside a block of RAM to hold data the system expects to access repeatedly. Access to RAM is quicker than access to fixed storage.

CAD: computer-aided design. A means of designing products with a computer. CAD users can manipulate design data through the keyboard, mouse, light pen, or other attached device.

Call: To transfer control to a specified routine.

CAM: Computer-aided manufacturing. A means of computer control in manufacturing processes.

Captive account: A VAX/VMS account with limited privileges. In some captive accounts, only certain commands of procedures are permitted.

Carrier signal: The base signal onto which information is modulated for transmission.

CCITT: Comite Consultatif International de Telegraphique et Telephonique (International Telegraph and Telephone Consultative Committee), a European communications standards committee.

Central office: A local telephone "exchange" or switching system that connects various "local loops" (communication links to customers) to other local central offices or to toll offices for long-distance communication.

Centrex: Service leased by telephone companies to larger users, performing at a central office the functions ordinarily undertaken by a private branch exchange (PBX).

Centronics parallel: A standard for parallel communication. See parallel communication.

Channel: In network terms, a logical path connecting a user process to a physical device unit, as assigned by the operating system. In telecommunications, a transmission path or circuit between two points.

Character: A symbol represented by an ASCII code.

Character buffer: The temporary storage area used by EDT and some other programs to hold the last deleted character.

Character code: An integer value representing a character. It can be generated by a single key on the keyboard or a combination of keys, including control keys.

Character cell: The pixel area on the screen used to display a single graphic character.

Character encoding: The method used by a terminal or a computer to encode information. Most current systems use 8-bit codes; other systems are based on a smaller 7-bit set.

Character key: A key that generates a keyboard event when pressed.

Character set: A hard character set is a design for a group of characters built into the internal memory of a terminal. Typical hard character sets include ASCII and DEC Supplemental Graphic sets. A soft character set is a group of characters downloaded to the terminal from a computer or other source.

Character string: A contiguous set of bytes. The computer identifies a character string by giving it two attributes: an address and a length. The address is the location of the byte holding the first character of the string. The length is the number of characters in the string, stored in subsequent bytes of increasing address.

Chip: An integrated circuit used as a microprocessor or a memory storage unit in microcomputers. The chip is constructed on a tiny silicon flake with gates and paths formed out of films of metal. Also called a microchip.

Cluster: A set of pages brought into memory in a single paging operation. Also, a configuration of VAX processors.

Coaxial cable: A design of media with a solid or stranded copper conductor surrounded by foam or plastic insulation, a woven copper or foil shield, and a rubber or plastic outer covering. A type of cable used in some computer networks as well as in cable television and in other applications. The copper braid or foil shield on the coaxial cable allows it to resist interference better than some other types of wiring, such as twisted pair.

COBOL: An abbreviation of common business oriented language. A high-level programming language often used for business applications.

Codec: A microchip for coding and decoding, used to produce digital output from analog signals, or vice versa.

Column: A vertical row of character positions on a screen. Most terminals can display 80 or 132 columns in width.

Command: An instruction requesting the computer to perform a defined action.

Command file: See command procedure.

Command interpreter: The element of the operating system that receives, checks for errors, and parses the commands sent by the user of a command file.

Command procedure: The file containing commands and any necessary data that the command interpreter can act upon as if the instructions had been typed in by the user.

Compatible: In hardware, the ability to work with or act in an identical manner to another piece of equipment. In software, the ability to interchange files or data without re-entering them from the keyboard.

Compatibility mode: A mode that permits the VAX's central processor to execute nonprivileged PDP-11 instructions, assuring compatibility with software intended for that earlier series of DEC machines. See also native mode.

Compiler: Computer software that translates a program written in a high-level language, such as BASIC, Pascal, COBOL, or C, into binary machine code. The program being translated is the source code, and the translated (compiled) result is called object code. Compiled programs generally run much faster than interpreted programs.

Compose character key: A key used to initiate display and transmission of certain special characters not part of the ordinary computer keyboard. Characters are sent by typing the compose character key and then one or two prespecified keyboard characters. On the LK201 keyboard used with VT220 and VT300 series terminals, a compose indicator illuminates while a compose character function is underway.

Compose sequence: See compose character key.

Composite video output connector: A connector on a VT terminal or other display device that provides a video output signal to drive an external slave display. Also called NTSC video (for National Television Standards Committee), this system sends information on brightness, color, and timing on a single wire. The resulting image is not as sharp as can be produced using an RGB system.

Concealed device: An I/O device that has been given a logical name. The user will use and see the logical name in most system commands and responses, rather than the device name.

Condition: An error state that exists when an exception occurs. See exception, and condition handler.

Condition handler: A procedure executed by the system when a process exception occurs. When the exception occurs, the computer will look for an appropriate condition handler and within the context of the situation, follow the instructions given there.

Configuration: The combination of various parts, options, and cards that makes up a computer system.

Configuration database: A database of files containing information about the system and network components.

Console: The control unit used by the system operator to start and stop the system, monitor system operation and perform diagnostics.

Console terminal: The hard-copy terminal connected to the central processor console.

Context switching: The act of interrupting the activity in progress and switching to another. The switching can be done by the system as it concludes one process and moves on to the next, or can be performed by the user in certain circumstances.

Control characters: A set of characters, not usually displayed on the screen, that make the terminal perform a specific function. Examples include CR (carriage return) and LF (line feed). Control characters can be generated by a program or by holding down the Control key (Ctrl) on the keyboard and typing another key. In effect, another shift key. Special signals can also be sent by using the Alt key in the same manner. In some applications manuals and on-screen displays, Ctrl is signified with the ^ symbol.

Control key: A computer keyboard key that works as another shift level, sending "control characters" to the computer for action. The command is issued by holding down the Ctrl key on the keyboard and then typing a second character. In this book, and in most application programs, a command calling for use of a control character would be printed as Ctrl-A.

Conversational Monitor System: See CMS.

Core: The center of a fiber optic cable, used to conduct light pulses generated by a laser or light-emitting diode (LED). Also a type of main memory in older computer systems.

CPU: Central processing unit. The "brain" of the computer, as opposed to ancillary units such as memory and storage.

CRC: Cyclical redundancy check. A form of error checking used during the transfer of data in I/O operations such as with disk drives and communications links.

Crossover cable: See null modem.

CSMA/CA, CSMA/CD: See carrier sense multiple access.

Ctrl: See Control key.

Cursor keys: The "arrow" keys on a terminal's keyboard used to move the cursor from point to point on the screen.

Cursor: A dash or block displayed on the screen of a terminal to indicate where the next alphanumeric character will appear. The cursor can be customized as part of the set-up choices on most VT terminals.

Cylinder: The set of all tracks on a disk that can be accessed without repositioning the read/write head.

Data flow control: A method of synchronizing communication between a terminal and its host system or printer.

Data link layer: The second layer of the OSI model, responsible for managing the flow of data from a network device to a receiving device, and ensuring that the information arrives safely.

dB: See decibel.

DC: Direct current. An electrical current that flows in one direction only.

DCL: Digital command language. A component of the VMS operating system through which the user can interact with the system to issue commands.

Debug: To repair operating problems in a piece of hardware or software.

DEC supplemental graphic character set: A set of 94 graphic characters including special characters such as letters with accents and diacritical marks used by European languages.

DEC multinational character set: The standard character set of the VT220 and VT300 series of terminals.

DEC special graphic character set: A group of characters with special symbols and line segments, as well as equivalents to many of the graphics characters of the ASCII character set. Also called the VT100 line drawing character set.

Decibel: A unit of measurement of the change in strength of a transmission signal. Calculated as a ratio between two amounts of electrical or acoustic signals.

Decryption: The process of restoring encoded information to its original, unencoded form.

Dedicated: An element of the system that is assigned to a single purpose or user.

Default: The ordinary or expected element of a command. The operating system will substitute, in most cases, the default value in a command unless some other information is provided.

Detached process: A process that has no owner. Such processes are created by the job controller when a user logs in, when a batch job is begun, or when a logical link connect is requested. Detached jobs can continue to operate even if the originating user is conducting other operations.

Device: Any peripheral unit connected to the processor for sending, receiving, or transmitting data. Devices include printers, terminals, mass storage devices such as magnetic disks and communication controllers, and modems. A device can be "pseudo" in that it is not real but exists only for the purposes of the system.

Device driver: Software associated with each device in the system that works as an interface between the operating system and the device controller.

Diacritical marks: Symbols that are used in some languages to call for a change in the standard pronunciation of a letter, such as acute (ʹ) and grave (ˋ) accents and the tilde (˜).

Diagnostic: A program to test hardware, logic, or memory and report any faults it finds.

Dialog box: In a window application, a displayed box that requests information to complete a command, or informs the user that the application is waiting for the completion of a process.

Digital: Data in the form of digits, a numerical representation of events or information. The other form of data manipulated by a computer is analog and is based on a wave or other form of analogy to the actual event.

Digital command language: The command interpreter in a VAX/VMS system.

Digital Switch: An electronic switch that can alter the channel routing of digital signals without converting them to analog signals.

Dimmed: On a window display, an element drawn in gray tones rather than black.

DIP switch: Abbreviation for dual in-line package; a type of multiple switch found on many computers and peripherals and used to make option or protocol selections.

Direct connect: A type of modem that plugs directly into the phone line jack. Compare to acoustic coupler.

Direct memory access: A means of transferring data between the main RAM storage and input/output devices that does not require involvement of the microprocessor and therefore operates at a faster rate.

Directory: A file that catalogs the files stored in a particular physical location. Included in most directories are the file name, type, and version number as well as a number that identifies the file's actual location and points to a list of its attributes.

Disable: To stop operation of a circuit or device; opposite of enable.

Dispersion: A gradual loss of integrity, or "blurring," of light pulse during transmission along a fiber optic cable.

Display attribute: On a video display, a property that can be assigned to all or part of a display. For example, a bit can be low-intensity, high-intensity, blinking, or a particular color.

DMA: See direct memory access.

Dot matrix: A family of printers that produce letters, numbers, and graphics through the use of dots drawn within a grid by a moving print head. Matrix printers can be impact or nonimpact.

Dot pitch: The closeness of one phosphor dot to another on a monitor screen. The smaller or finer the dot pitch, the sharper the image. An ordinary television set typically has a dot pitch of about 0.62 millimeters, a high-resolution monitor is usually rated at 0.40 millimeters or less, and a medium-resolution device falls in between.

Double precision: A system of storage of numbers inside a computer that extends the value out to two computer words. See single precision.

Download: (Also called down-line load). The movement of data or instructions from the host to the terminal. Contrast to upload.

Downloadable character set: (Also called down-line loadable character set, or soft character set). A set of characters downloaded to a terminal from the host system to supplement or replace the built-in, or "hard" character set of the terminal.

DRCS: Dynamically redefinable character set. See downloadable character set.

Drive: The mechanical element of a mass storage unit. A magnetic tape or disk, for example, is mounted on a drive.

Driver: The code and data that oversees the physical input and output of data to a device. A set of instructions in a software package that operates a particular piece of hardware, such as a printer or plotter. See device driver.

Duplex: Simultaneous, independent transmission of data in both directions on a data communications channel. A single direction system is called half-duplex.

Dvorak keyboard: A keyboard layout said to allow speedier typing than that permitted by the familiar QWERTY keyboard. Some manufacturers offer replacement keyboards for the PC family, and there are also software fixes to convert the standard keyboard to a different layout.

Dynamic RAM: Memory using transistors and capacitors as storage elements, and therefore requiring a recharge (refresh) every few milliseconds. Memory that does not require a refresh is called static memory.

EBCDIC: Extended binary coded decimal interchange code. A set of 6-bit characters used to represent data in some IBM systems. Includes all 51 COBOL characters. Compare to ASCII.

Echo: A characteristic of a communications setup that calls for characters typed by the user on the keyboard to be also displayed on the screen or printer.

Echoplex: A protocol that has the receiving station echo back each character to the transmitting station as a check on proper communication.

Editing keypad: The supplemental keypad on some terminals designed to allow easy entry of editing commands, including cursor and page movement and insertion or deletion of characters.

EIA host port connector: A port on the back of a VT terminal used to connect the device to a host computer either directly or through the use of a modem.

Emulation: The ability of one piece of hardware or software to act like another. For example, the VT320 terminal can emulate the earlier VT220 or VT100 series of terminals if required by a particular software application. Or, a PC can run software allowing it to emulate the dissimilar VT220 series of terminals in a direct connection or a telecommunications session.

Emulators: Devices or software that allows one computer or piece of telecommunications equipment to mimic another. This allows the mixing of machines from different companies or of different internal architectures, and also allows one machine to have more than one use.

Enable: To allow a device or circuit to operate. Contrast with disable.

Encryption: The process of encoding information so that it is not easily understood by persons or devices without a copy of the decryption code.

EPROM: Erasable programmable read-only memory. See ROM.

Error messages: Information from the program or from the operating system informing the user of a problem in the program or the machine.

Esc: The "Escape" character, used to initiate an escape sequence.

Escape sequence: A special command to the system. The sequence begins with the ESC character and is transmitted without interpretation to the software or operating system for action.

Ethernet: A network protocol and cabling scheme used by Digital Equipment Corp., 3Com, and other manufacturers. Originally developed by Xerox.

Event: An occurrence that an application may be called upon to respond to.

Exception: An event detected by the hardware or software that effects a change in the normal execution of instructions. Examples would include attempts to perform a privileged or reserved instruction and arithmetic traps such as overflow, underflow, and division by 0. When an event occurs that is completely outside of the current instruction, it is called an interrupt.

Executable image: An image that can be run in a process.

Executive: The collection of procedures in the operating system to provide the basic control and monitoring functions.

Executive mode: A highly privileged processor access mode used for many of the operating system's service procedures.

Exit: An activity that occurs when an image execution is terminated, either normally or abnormally. The system de-assigns I/O channels and other assignments made for the purpose of the image.

Exit handler: A procedure executed when an image exits.

Fault: A hardware exception condition that occurs in the middle of an instruction, leaving the computer's internal registers and memory in such a state that eliminating the fault and restarting the instruction will give correct results.

Femtosecond: A unit of time measurement for high-speed laser blinks. One unit is equal to a millionth of a billionth (1/1,000,000,000,000,000) of a second.

Fiber optics: A cable made of fiber glass strands that transmits data in the form of pulses of light instead of pulses of electricity.

Field: A set of contiguous bytes in a logical record.

FIFO: First-in, first-out. The order in which processing is ordinarily performed. In other words, the computer will act upon the oldest command in its queue before coming to the most recently added command. See also LIFO.

File: Any named, stored program, or data.

File control block: An element of the operating system where information about the access path for files is stored.

File header: A block in an index file describing a file with information needed by the system to find and use the file.

File locking: A means of protecting shared data from corruption by preventing simultaneous read/write access to two users or two programs.

File name: The identification of a file, employed by the user in retrieving and storing a file. On a VAX/VMS system, the file name can be as many as 39 alphanumeric characters in length.

File name extension: See file type.

File server: A computer on a network dedicated in full or part to storage of files in private or shared directories or subdirectories.

File sharing: The capability of a relative or indexed file to allow access to more than one process.

File specification: The unique name of a file. On a VAX/VMS system, the file specification identifies the node, device, directory name, file type, and version number.

File type: On a VAX/VMS system, the field of a file specification to identify a particular class of files, such as compiler, assembly, data, and listings. Can be as many as 39 alphanumeric characters in length.

Files-11:   The disk structure used by the VAX/VMS operating system as well as some other Digital systems. VMS uses Files-11 structure level 2, but also supports level 1 for compatibility with earlier systems.

Filter: A procedure of some operating systems that allows the operating system to read input (usually from a file) and then process it into a different form.

Firmware: Instructions to the computer that are encoded in a chip. Contrast to software, which has instructions stored at first on a disk or cartridge and is later transferred to the volatile internal memory of the computer for execution.

Flip-flop: A circuit or device in which active elements are capable of assuming either of two stable states with the application of electrical current.

Floating point data: On a VAX/VMS system, a single precision floating point number 4 bytes in length, having a range from plus or minus 2.910^{-37} to plus or minus 1.710^{38} and a precision of approximately seven decimal digits. See also G-floating data and H-floating data.

Font: A style or design for characters to appear on a screen or to be created by a printer.

Form feed: On a printer, the movement of the paper to the top of the next sheet of continuous-form paper. In the EDT word processor of a VAX/VMS system, the movement of the cursor position to the start of a new page.

Formatting: The preparation of a disk for writing and reading data by marking it off into pie-wedges called sectors and concentric circles called tracks. There are several different formatting schemes and they are generally not compatible with each other.

FORTRAN: A programming language often used for scientific applications. Abbreviation for Formula Translation.

Frame: A packet of information on a token-ring network; Also, in serial communication, the elapsed time from the start bit to the last stop bit.

Frequency: In an electrical signal, the number of waves within the signal in each second of time. Measured in Hertz. The range of frequencies allowed for a signal determines its bandwidth.

Frequency-shift keying (FSK): A means of modulation used in 300-baud modems that uses one frequency to represent 0s and another for 1s. See also phase-shift keying.

FSK: See frequency-shift keying.

Full-duplex: A mode of data communication between two devices in which signals can travel in both directions at the same time. For example, voice communication over a telephone is full-duplex. See also half-duplex.

Function key: A keyboard character that can be temporarily or permanently assigned to perform a certain task when struck.

G-floating data: In a VAX/VMS system, an extended range floating point number 8 bytes in length, having a range of plus or minus 0.5610^{-308} to plus or minus 0.910^{308} and a precision of approximately 15 decimal digits. See also floating point data and H-floating data.

Gateway: An intelligent device that bridges between networks running incompatible protocols. A link from one network to another network. An internal office local area network, for example, could have a gateway to an external public communications network for transmission of electronic mail to outside addresses. One public information network could also have a gateway that allows its subscribers to tie into the offerings of a different system without having to sign off the original network.

Generic device name: A device name that identifies the type of device but not a particular unit.

Gigabit: One billion binary digits.

Gigabyte: One billion 8-bit computer words.

Global: Affecting the entire file, system, or image, depending upon the context. In a text file, a global replacement would be to change all instances of a particular string of characters to something else.

Global section: A shareable image section that can be made available to all processes in a system. Access is set by privilege.

Global symbol: A symbol that can be made to extend across a number of files or strings. The linker resolves, or matches, references with definitions.

Gold key: A special key on a VAX terminal keyboard enabling alternate key functions. Used within WPS, EDT, and many other programs.

Graphic characters: A set of alphanumeric characters that can be displayed on the screen of a terminal.

Group: A set of users who have been given special access privileges to each others' directories and files, unless the files have been specifically protected. VMS organizes users under the following hierarchy: system/owner/group/world.

H-floating data: In a VAX/VMS system, an extended range floating point number 16 bytes in length, having a range of plus or minus 0.8410^{-4932} to plus or minus 0.5910^{4932} and a precision of approximately 33 decimal digits. See also G-floating data and floating point data.

Half-duplex: A mode of data communication that allows signals to travel in only one direction at a time. For example, a walkie-talkie radio or a desktop intercom may be half-duplex in operation. See also full-duplex.

Handshaking: A protocol that consists of predefined signals to control the interchange of data and maintenance of a link.

Hanging: Slow response of the system because of a heavy load of users or compute-intensive jobs.

Hard character set: One of the sets of characters built into a terminal as a default design. Contrast to downloadable character sets, also called soft character sets.

Hard-copy terminal: Terminals that print on paper rather than display on a video screen.

Help screens: Assistance to the user available from within an applications program. Some packages allow you to adjust the amount of help that will appear on your screen so that once you know a system you no longer have to go through unnecessary prompting.

Hexadecimal: A numbering system based on 16, as opposed to the decimal system base of 10 and the binary system base of 2. The letters A through F are used to indicate the numbers 10 through 15.

Hibernation: A process made inactive, but known to the system. The system keeps track of the process's current status and can recall the process on the basis of a predefined wake request or a command from another process or the user. See also suspension.

Hierarchical network: A communications system designed to include various stages of signal routing and multiplexing for better efficiency in transmission.

High bit: A system used by some word processors, including WordStar, and some other programs, in which certain characters in storage are given a value higher than their ordinary ASCII character value. High-bit characters are used in WordStar, for example, to indicate to the program the ends of each word so that microjustification can be accomplished. In order to interchange files from a high-bit program to a standard ASCII program or to DOS, a high-bit stripper utility is often used.

High-level language: A human language-like means of communicating with the computer to give commands or create a program. Higher-level languages do not include machine specific commands that directly address a computer, such as those in assembly and machine languages. High-level languages are translated into machine code by an interpreter or compiler before running or at the time of execution.

Highlighting: The display of characters, blocks, and other screen markers in a brighter-than-ordinary form. Some systems use color, underlining, or dimming as a means of identifying blocks or characters.

Hold screen: This key freezes the screen display and stops any other characters coming in from the host computer from being displayed. This function is useful when viewing a lengthy directory or file that would otherwise scroll off the screen before it could be read. The Hold Screen key is a "toggle"—pressing it once turns the mode on; pressing it a second time turns the mode off. On the LK201 and similar keyboards, a "hold screen indicator" is illuminated when the freeze has been initiated.

Holder: A user with a particular identifier.

Home: Usually defined as the top-left corner of the screen or the active window of a screen.

Horizontal scroll: The shifting of the screen to the right to display text that is beyond the ordinary 80-column borders of a monitor.

Host: The computer or terminal server that a terminal communicates with.

Host node: Under DECnet, the host node is the node that provides services to another node.

Icon: In a window environment, a graphic symbol that stands for a system resource or procedure. A drawing of a file folder may represent a data file to be opened or processed, for example; some systems use a garbage can to represent a delete or throw-away operation.

Identifier: The signification of a user or group of users to the system. VMS has three types of identifiers: UIC identifiers, system-defined identifiers, and general identifiers.

Image: The procedures and data bound together by the linker. VMS has three types of images: executable, shareable, and system.

Image name: The name of the file in which an image is stored.

Image privileges: The privileges held by an image once installed.

Initialize: A procedure usually undertaken at the start of a session or a new program module to set counters, switches, or addresses to 0 or to a particular value. In some operating systems, to initialize means to format a disk.

Input stream: From the computer's point of view, the source of commands and data—the user's terminal, a batch stream, or a command procedure.

Insert: To add a character, word, line, or block to a file.

Instruction: An expression in a programming language that specifies a single operation. An instruction set comprises the series of instructions that gives guidance to a piece of hardware.

Integer: Any whole number, including zero, either negatively or positively signed.

Integrated circuit: A complete electronic circuit formed on a microchip.

Integrated optical circuit: Optical equivalent of a microelectronic circuit to generate, detect, switch and transmit light in lightwave communications systems and expected optical computers.

Integrated services digital network: See ISDN.

Interactive: A system in which the user and the operating system communicate directly with the operating system acting upon commands and requests immediately.

Interface: The connection between two pieces of equipment.

Interrupt: The suspension of an operation caused by an event external to that process and performed in such a way that the process can later be resumed. For example, striking a key on the keyboard can be an interrupt to a particular program. See also exceptions.

ISDN: Integrated services digital network. A plan for a hierarchy of digital transmission and switching systems, synchronized so that all digital elements work together for transmission of voice, data, and video signals. A true ISDN will do away with the need for modems since the circuit will be able to carry and switch digital signals directly from computers without the need for an analog intermediary signal.

ISO: International Standards Organization, promulgator of the Open System Interconnection (OSI) model.

Job: A record maintained by the computer to track a process and any subprocesses. Jobs can be either batch or interactive.

Journal file: Under an EDT editing session in a VAX/VMS system, a file that records all of the data and commands sent to the computer during one session. Can be used to reconstruct a file lost in an interrupted session.

K: Short for kilo, used as a unit of measure of memory and storage. The value of K is 2^{10}, or 1,024, although it is commonly used to express a value of 1,000.

Keyword: A command name, qualifier, or option.

Kilobit: Informally, one thousand binary bits. A kilobit is actually 1,024 bits.

Kilobyte: Informally, one thousand bytes. A kilobyte is actually 1,024 bytes.

Kilohertz: One thousand cycles per second of electrical frequency.

Label: A record that identifies a mass storage unit volume or file section.

LAN: See local area network.

Laser: An electronic device that can produce light, within a very narrow frequency spectrum, as rapid pulses. Semiconductor-controlled lasers can operate at pulse rates of billions of "blinks" per second. See also femtoseconds. Compare to LED.

Least-significant digit: The rightmost or low-order digit of a number.

LED: Light-emitting diode. A solid-state electronic device that can produce light, within a broad frequency spectrum, as rapid pulses for short-distance transmission on fiber-optic cable. Compare to laser.

LIFO: Last-in, first-out. The order in which commands are processed. Under this scheme, the most recently entered command is acted on first. See also FIFO.

Light-emitting diode: See LED.

Light pen: A device used to communicate position to a computer by shining the light at a CRT screen or touching the screen.

Limit: The maximum size or number of resources allowed a particular job, as assigned by the system operator. See also quota.

Line printer: A hard-copy output device that prints a single line at a time at very high speed.

Linker: A program that creates an executable program, referred to as an image, from one or more object modules produced by a language compiler or assembler. Programs must be linked before they can be executed.

LK201: The standard keyboard used by Digital with its VT220 and VT300 series of terminals.

Local area network (LAN): An interconnection of computers for the exchange of data and programs and the shared use of peripherals including printers and storage devices.

Local controller mode: Used to direct the keystrokes of a terminal in local mode to a directly connected printer. The mode is initiated from within the set-up series of menus by selecting local mode from the main menu and then printer controller mode from the printer set-up menu. See printing modes for other conditions.

Local loop: In telephonic communication, local transmission lines that connect subscribers to the central switching office of a telephone company.

Local mode: The condition that exists when a terminal is set up as an off-line device in direct communication with a printer or other device. Contrast with on-line mode.

Lock: A software command that blocks unauthorized users from reading or writing to a file. Can be used to protect the integrity of a file in use by several persons at the same time. It can also be used as part of a security system to prevent unauthorized access to sensitive material.

Locked password: A password that cannot be changed by the owner of the account, but only by the system operator.

Log: A record of performance.

Logging in: The process of identifying a user to the system. The user types in an account name and a password in response to prompts from the system. If the account name and password are registered in the system, the user will be given access to that account and all of its privileges.

Logging out: Signing off a VMS account after work is completed.

Logical name: A name, assigned by the user, as a substitute for part or all of a file specification.

Login file: A command file containing instructions automatically executed at login.

LOGO: A programming language valued as an educational tool.

Longword: In a VAX/VMS system, four contiguous bytes (32 bits), with bits numbered from 0 to 31, right to left. The address of the longword is the address of the byte containing bit 0. When interpreted as a number, a longword is a two's complement integer (bit 31 is the sign bit in a signed integer). As a signed bit, a longword ranges from $-2,147,483,648$ to $2,147,483,647$. As an unsigned integer, the longword ranges in value from 0 to $4,294,967,295$.

Loop: See local loop.

Loopback: A diagnostic procedure for telecommunications in which a test message is sent from a transmitter and sent back by the receiver to be compared with the original message.

LU: Logical unit, or the port through which users communicate in an SNA network.

MAC: Media access control. See access protocol.

Mac: Shortened form of Macintosh, as in Apple Computer Company's Macintosh computer family.

Machine language: Instructions that can be operated upon directly, without the use of an interpreter. Each brand and sometimes each model within a company's line usually uses its own machine language code.

Macro: A statement that commands a language processor to generate a predefined set of instructions for action by the system.

Macroprocessor: A program or utility that overlays a portion of an operating system to interpret and expand upon keystrokes or other input. For example, a keyboard macroprocessor could be used to redefine single characters to stand for lengthy strings.

Mailbox: A software equivalent of a physical mailbox used for communication between VMS users. Users can address mail to a particular mailbox, and recipients open their mailbox to retrieve messages.

MAP: Manufacturing automation protocol. A factory-floor network protocol based on a token-passing design, promoted by General Motors Corp.

Mass storage device: An input/output device for the storage of data and other files while not in active use by the system. Such devices include magnetic disks, magnetic tapes, optical disks, and floppy disks.

Mbyte: See megabyte.

Media: Cabling or wiring used to carry signals on a network, including coaxial, twisted-pair, and fiber optic cabling.

Megabit: An Mbit is technically 1,000 kilobits, or 1,048,576 bits. In common usage often taken as 1 million bits.

Megabyte: An Mbyte is technically 1,000 kilobytes, or 1,048,576 bytes. In common usage often taken as 1 million bytes.

Memory: Physical locations into which data or instructions can be placed. Each location has an address to allow the system to locate it.

Memory limited: A program that will only allow files as large as the available space in the computer's memory, not allowing swapping of portions of the file to disk. Compare to virtual memory.

Menu: A list of choices that can be selected through the use of a cursor or mouse-controlled pointer.

Microsecond: A unit of time measurement equal to one millionth of a second.

Microwave: In communications, an atmospheric transmission method using high radio frequencies, in the gigahertz (GHz) bands. Used to transmit analog or digital voice, data or video signals.

Modem: Short for modulator-demodulator. A device which translates (modulates) digital impulses from a computer into analog waves for transmission over telephone lines or other communications media. At the receiving end, the analog signal is converted back (demodulated) to a digital signal.

Modified frequency modulation (MFM): A magnetic recording process that varies the amplitude (height) and frequency of the "write" signal. Used in many disk drives.

Modulate: The alteration of a carrier signal in such a manner as to impress upon it information that can be demodulated at the other end into pure data. Most common forms of modulation are by means of altering amplitude, frequency, or phase angle of a signal.

Module: In software, a portion of a program or a program library. In hardware, a physical element of a computer, as in logic module.

Most-significant digit: The leftmost nonzero digit of a number. Also called the high-order position. Its opposite is the least-significant digit.

Motherboard: The main circuit board of a computer, including the microprocessor and some memory. Also called a system board. Secondary boards are sometimes called daughter boards.

Mouse: A small device that can be held in the hand or moved on a desktop to position a cursor on the screen. Used in graphics and as a substitute for cursor keys. Buttons on the top of the mouse can also be used to transmit commands when the cursor is in the desired location.

Multicast addressing: A mode of addressing in which a message is sent to a group of predefined nodes.

Multicast group address: An address given to a group of nodes on an Ethernet and used in multicast addressing to send a message to that group.

Multimode fiber: In lightwave systems, an optical fiber designed with a relatively large core that allows connection to light sources, such as LEDs, that are larger in frequency than lasers. Compare to single-mode fiber.

Multinational character set: A set of characters that goes beyond the ASCII 8-bit character set to include international alphanumeric characters, including characters with diacritical marks and special symbols.

Multiplexer: A device that combines a number of communications channels to allow them to share a common circuit. In an analog system, frequency-division multiplexing is usually employed. In a digital system, time-division multiplexing is usually employed.

MVS/TSO (Multiple virtual storage/time-sharing option):   A time-sharing version of MVS.

MVS (multiple virtual storage):   An IBM operating system that allows several users to use the mainframe as if it were dedicated to each of their uses alone.

Nanosecond: A billionth of a second. Abbreviated as n.

Native image: An image whose instructions are executed in native mode.

Native mode: The ordinary and primary mode of execution for a VAX processor. Under this definition, programmed instructions are interpreted as byte-aligned, variable-length instructions that operate on four data types: byte, word, longword, and quadword integers; floating and double floating character strings; packed decimals; and variable-length bit fields. See also compatibility mode.

NCP (network control program):   A resident program on some IBM devices to control routing, transmission, and packaging of data.

NetBIOS: Software that links a network to specific hardware. The original NetBIOS was developed by IBM, although other vendors have created equivalents.

Network: A scheme that connects separate computer systems for the interchange of data and other tasks.

Network file system: A protocol, originally developed by Sun Microsystems, that allows computers and workstations on a network to use the files and attached peripherals of another computer on the network as if they were local.

Network layer: The third layer of the OSI model, including the rules for determination of pathways for data on a network.

Node: An individual computer system in a network.

Node address: The unique, numeric identification required for each node in a network.

Node name: An optional alphanumeric identification for a node.

Non-Volatile RAM: Computer memory that is able to retain data even after power to the system is shut off. Such RAM is used in many terminals to store configuration settings selected through use of the set-up series of menus.

Normal mode: The standard printing mode that allows all keyboard printing functions, including print screen, to be initiated from the keyboard. See printing modes for other conditions.

NTSC video: See composite video.

Null: The ASCII character with a binary value of 000. In programming, a null is an absence of information. The character is used to fill a storage space or to consume a specific amount of time. A null character can be inserted into a sequence of characters without affecting the meaning of the sequence.

Null modem: A special cable to link two identical input/output ports on computers. The key element is the crossing of the transmit and receive wires so that the output of one machine goes to the input of the other. Also called a cross-over cable or a modem eliminator.

Numeric keypad: A supplemental keypad on some terminals intended for rapid entry of numbers and punctuation marks. Can also be redefined to the special needs of a particular application program to allow quick entry of special commands.

NVR: See non-volatile RAM.

Object: A process that is the recipient of a logical link request, called upon to perform a specific network function or a user-defined image for a special purpose. In hardware, an object refers to a system resource such as a file or device.

Object code: See compiler.

Object module: The output of a language processor such as an assembler or compiler, in binary code, used as input to a linker.

Octal number: A number in the base-8 numbering system, which uses the numerals 0 to 7 only. Octal numbering is used in certain applications because it is easy to convert to the binary numbers actually used by the computer.

Offset address: See address.

On-line mode: The condition that exists when a terminal is set up to communicate with a host computer. Off-line modes include local and set-up. See also operational states.

Open account: An account that does not require a password for access.

Open system interconnection: See OSI.

Operating system: A set of programs that control the execution of computer programs, oversee system functions, and handle the interactive communication with the user.

Operational states: Conditions of operation for a terminal, including on-line for communications with a host computer; local for operations not intended to be transmitted to a host computer, and set-up for use of the terminal's built-in customization program.

Operator: The person responsible for maintenance of a computer system and the accounts of users.

Optical computer: A design for a computer system that will operate with photons instead of electrons. Scientists believe an optical computer could be as much as 1,000 times faster than current electronic computers.

Optical waveguide: A solid glass fiber for transmission of communications signals generated by lasers or LEDs. Also called a lightguide.

OSI: Open system interconnection. A network model promulgated by the International Standards Organization intended to allow interconnection of heterogeneous computers and networks.

Out-of-band signaling: A system using bandwidth for control signaling that is outside the normal voice or data bandwidth. An example is the "D" channel of the ISDN basic rate interface.

Output file: A file that contains the results of an operation.

Owner: A member of a group to which a file, global section, or mailbox belongs. See also group and world.

PABX: See PBX.

Packed decimal: Because decimal digits require only four bits for expression, two digits can be stored in a single byte using this method.

Packet switching: A scheme to more efficiently use a transmission channel by switching addressed packets in and out of the channel only as needed.

Packet: A unit of data to be routed from a source node to a destination node. Typically also includes the identification of the sending and intended receiving nodes and error detection information.

Page: In programming terms, a set of 512 contiguous byte locations used as the unit of memory mapping and protection.

Page fault: An exception generated by a reference to a page that is not in the working set of the process.

Paging: To bring pages of an executing process into physical memory when referenced, a process at the heart of the definition of the VAX (virtual address extended) architecture. When a process executes, all of its pages are placed in "virtual memory." Only the pages in active use, though, need to reside in physical memory; the remaining pages reside on disk until they are needed in physical memory. Under VAX/VMS, a process is paged when it references more pages than it is allowed in its working set or when it first activates an image in memory. If the process refers to a page not in its working set, a page fault occurs, which causes the operating system to read in the referenced pages from wherever they are located.

Parallel communications: Transmission of information over a pathway consisting of several wires, allowing the sending of more than one bit at a time.

Parity: A setting in serial communications that requires that the number of bits in each word of transmitted data be even or odd. Used as part of the error-checking process.

Parity bit: In data communications, a bit that carries parity information to help verify that received data matches transmitted data.

Parity checking: In RAM, a system used by many computers that checks the integrity of data stored in memory by adding up the value of each of the eight bits that make up a computer word and then determining whether the total is odd or even. The answer is then stored in a separate chip on the computer and regularly compared with the memory. If a mechanical or electrical error causes one bit to change in memory, the parity readings will differ and a parity error will be communicated to the operating system.

Parity error: A condition that results when the parity bit received by a device does not match the data.

Parsing: Breaking a command string into its various elements to interpret it for action.

Pascal: A structured programming language named for the French mathematician Blaise Pascal.

Passwords: Character strings entered by the user and examined by the operating system to validate access to the system.

Patch: A change made in the assembly language code of a program.

PBX: Private branch exchange. An automated switching system for a private telephone system for an office. Available in both analog and digital systems, digital models can switch both data and voice signals.

Peer-to-peer: A network design that allows any connected computer to make available to the network its resources while also running local applications.

Peripheral devices: Any hardware, excluding the CPU and physical memory, that provides input or accepts output from the system. Peripherals include printers, terminals, and disk drives.

Photodetector: In a lightwave system, a device used to turn pulses of light into bursts of electricity. Used at the receiving end of a lightwave system to convert light pulses into a signal that can be directly used by the computer.

Photon: The fundamental unit of light. Photons are to optical fibers what electrons are to copper wires.

Physical address: To the computer, the address used by hardware to identify a specific location in physical memory or on-line secondary storage such as a disk drive. In network terms, the physical address is the unique address of a specific system on an Ethernet circuit.

Physical layer: The first layer of the OSI model, defining network wiring and electrical standards.

Physical memory: The main, internal memory of the computer.

PID: Process identification.

Pixel: Picture element, the smallest unit of display on a video screen, used to create graphic characters and graphic displays.

Primary password: The first user password requested from the user. Some systems may ask for a secondary password.

Port: A connector on a terminal to allow communication with a host or another device. Computers will typically have parallel or serial ports for devices such as modems, keyboards, monitors, printers, and plotters as well as networks.

Precision: A measure of the exactness of a number, based on the number of significant digits.

Presentation layer: The sixth layer of the OSI model, where data is formatted for screen display. Terminal emulators, which can make one type of device look like an entirely different device, typically do their work here.

Primary password: The first user password requested from the user. Some systems may ask for a secondary password.

Primary processor: The main processor in certain types of VAX computers. This processor handles input and output, scheduling, paging, and other system management functions. Such a system may have a secondary processor, called an attached processor, for other assignments.

Primary rate interface (PRI): A format within ISDN consisting of 23 "B" channels, each operating at 64 kilobits per second, and one "D" channel, operating at 64 kilobits per second. PRI is the next higher stage about BRI, the basic rate interface.

Print queue: A feature of an operating system that stores files to be printed in a queue similar to a print spooler.

Print server: A computer on the network dedicated in full or part to managing incoming and outgoing printing tasks. The server may maintain a print spooler and queue.

Printer buffer: See buffer.

Printer controller mode: In this condition, selectable from within the print menu of the set-up menu series, the host computer has direct control of a locally connected printer. Characters sent by the host computer go directly to the printer and are not displayed on the screen. Ordinary printer control functions cannot be initiated from the keyboard while the terminal is in this mode. See printing modes for other conditions.

Printer port connector: A port on a VT terminal used to connect a printer directly to the terminal.

Printing mode: See normal mode; auto print mode; printer controller mode; local controller mode.

Priority: The rank assigned to a process to allow the system to manage multiple requests for system resources.

Private branch exchange: See PBX.

Private section: An image section of a process that is not open for sharing among processes. Contrast with global section.

Privileged: Elements of the operating system that are restricted to the use of the system itself or to specific groups of users.

Process: The context within which an image executes.

Process identification (PID): A unique numerical value assigned by the computer to allow location and tracking of a process. Processes are assigned both process identification and a process name.

Process name: An alphanumeric string used to identify processes executing under the same group number. See also process identification.

Process priority: The operating system recognizes 32 levels of priority for scheduling purposes.

Process privileges: The privileges granted to a process by the system, a combination of user privileges and image privileges.

Program: A group of instructions intended to produce a particular result. See also image.

PROM: Programmable read-only memory.

Prompt: The system's indication to the user that it expects input.

Protection: The attributes assigned to a resource that limit the type of access for users.

Protocol: A set of rules defining a communications link.

Public switched network: A communications system, open to any subscriber, linking telephones and other devices.

Quadword: On a VAX/VMS system, four contiguous words, 64 bits in total, with bits numbered from 0 to 63, right to left. The address of the quadword is the address of the byte containing bit 0. When interpreted as a number, a quadword is a two's complement integer (bit 63 is the sign bit in a signed integer). As a signed bit, a quadword ranges from 2^{-63} to 2^{63}.

Qualifier: The element of a command that modifies the command through selection of an option. For example, in the command DIR/FULL the /FULL qualifier asks for a detailed listing of information about files, rather than the short form that is the default yielded by the unmodified command.

Queue: An ordered list of jobs to be processed. Jobs are generally performed in first-in, first-out (FIFO) order, but jobs can also be placed in different order on the basis of priority assigned them.

Quota: The amount of a system resource that a job is permitted to use in a particular period of time.

QWERTY: The keyboard layout used in the United States and most of the western world. Named after the first six letters at the top-left side of the keyboard. See also Dvorak keyboard.

RAM: Random access memory, accessible in any order by the computer. RAM is usually volatile, meaning that when the electrical power to the circuit is shut off, the information retained in RAM is erased.

RAM disk: A segment of RAM set aside and "formatted" so as to imitate a physical disk in a disk drive. The memory can be used as an additional disk drive for storage while the computer is in use, adding utility and speed. The information, though, must be copied to a real disk before the power is shut off. Other names for RAM disk include electronic disk, virtual disk, pseudo-disk, and super drive.

Random access: A memory or storage device on which all information is equally accessible at one time. Contrast with a serial storage device such as a reel of tape in which the retrieval time for any one bit depends upon the location of the bit last retrieved.

Raster: The pattern of horizontal lines on a video monitor scanned by the electron beam and selectively illuminated to form dots used to make up letters, numbers, or other images.

Raster fill: The process undertaken by a graphics camera or a specialized high-resolution monitor to fill in the spaces between raster lines of a video screen so as to produce a more finished appearance in a photograph.

Raster scan: Generating an image on a monitor or on a dot-matrix printer by translating the bit map in computer memory into coordinates for a cathode ray tube or a printer head.

Read-only memory: See ROM.

Read/write heads: The recording heads inside a disk drive.

Real-time process: A process that responds to particular events as they occur, rather than when the computer is ready to respond to them. Examples include laboratory and manufacturing process control. Contrast to batch processing.

Record: A set of related data, usually organized into fields.

Record length: The size of a record, in bytes.

Redirection: Under some operating systems, a command can be made to take input from a source other than the keyboard. For example, redirection could cause input from a file or from another piece of hardware. Similarly, output can be redirected away from the standard goal of the display and instead be sent to a file or other device.

Redirector: Software resident at most stations on a network that captures local requests for file and peripheral use and routes them onto the network.

Refresh memory: The area of computer memory that holds values indicating whether a particular dot of a graphics raster is off or on. The memory may also contain information on color and brightness.

Regenerators: Devices used along digital transmission paths to reshape and retime a digital signal. In a lightwave system, optoelectronic modules "refresh" light pulses blurred by dispersion during transmission.

Register: A storage device with a specified capacity such as a bit, a byte, a word, and so forth.

Remote device: A device not directly connected to the local node but available through a VAXcluster.

Remote file service: A form of distributed file system network protocols allowing sharing of network facilities as if they were local. Developed by ATT and part of most implementations of UNIX.

Repeaters: Amplifiers with electrical continuity to the cable to which they are connected. Signals enter one side of the amplifier and come out the other side stronger but with no switching or alteration. See also buffered repeaters.

Resolution: The number of pixels in a particular area determines resolution on a monitor. The greater the number of pixels per area, the greater the resolution.

Resource: A physical element of a computer system such as a device or memory.

Resume: To reactivate a suspended process. Contrast with wake.

Return key: On a computer, the Return key can serve several different functions, depending upon the application program in use and the particular context in which it is employed. In a word processor, the Return key generates a carriage return and linefeed command, as would be used at the end of a paragraph. It can also be used to "Enter" a command for action.

Reverse video: The ability of some terminals to reverse video contrast from, for example, white letters on a black background to black letters on a white background.

RFS: See remote file service.

RGB video: An acronym for a red/green/blue signal. Each of the color signals has its own transmitter and receiver and its own wire. More information can be transmitted and the resolution of an RGB monitor can be considerably greater than that of a composite monitor.

Ring: A form of network topology in which each station is connected to another unit to the "left" and "right" as if it were in a circle. Messages are passed through every station in turn but are retrieved only by the designated node.

ROM: Read only memory. Blocks of memory with instructions for the computer or operating system that can be read by the computer, but which can not be changed by the user or the system. Usually contains instructions and decoding information. ROMs are produced by designers in a single form. A PROM is a Programmable ROM that can be changed or updated. Forms of PROMS include the EPROM, which is erasable through the use of ultraviolet light. An EEPROM is an electrically erasable PROM that can be changed by sending an electrical signal.

Round robin: A type of time sharing that gives equal access to the CPU for images of equal priority. Each process at a given priority level executes in turn before any other process at the level.

Router: A dedicated machine in certain networks that reads the destination of a message and then determines the best route to that destination. See also network layer.

Run-time procedure library: The collection of procedures available to native-mode images at run time.

RS-232C: A set of standards for mechanical and electrical design of an interface typically used for serial (asynchronous) communications in microcomputers. The interface includes a connector with 25 pins, each of which is lettered and provides a specific function. Although the standard is claimed by many manufacturers, it is still necessary to ensure that any two claimed RS-232C devices use standard pin assignments and cable construction in order to communicate properly.

SAA: See systems application architecture.

Scroll: To move the window of text up or down, left or right to see more of the copy.

Scrolling: The movement of text on a video screen from bottom to top or top to bottom as new information is displayed.

SDLC: See Synchronous Data Link Control.

Secondary password: A password that may be asked of the user at login time after the primary password has been accepted.

Sectors: The pie-wedge segments of a formatted disk. See formatting.

Segment: A divided part of an application; not all segments need to be loaded into memory at the same time.

Serial communications: A method of arranging data bits of a byte to follow one another down a cable, as opposed to parallel communications in which each of the bits of a byte travels alongside each other in a multiple wire cable. See also asynchronous communications.

Serial communications controller: A single chip or group of chips and associated circuitry that handles serial input/output.

Served device: A device available to other nodes on a VAX-cluster.

Session layer: The fifth layer of the OSI model, responsible for setting the conditions under which individual nodes can communicate with each other.

Set-up menus. The selection of customization menus for terminals, accessible by the user. See also operational states.

Set-up mode: The condition that exists when a terminal is set up to use its built-in customization program. See also operational states and set-up menus.

Shareable image: An image that must be linked with one or more object modules in order to produce an executable image.

Signal-to-noise ratio: The power relationship between a communications signal and "noise"—unwanted disturbances or interferences—within the transmission bandwidth.

Significant digits: The digits in a number from the leftmost digit that is not a zero to the rightmost digit declared to be relevant. The numbers 3789, 0.003789, and 3.789 all have four significant digits.

Single-mode fiber: An optical fiber designed with a slender core capable of transmitting a narrow band of light frequencies, as generated by a laser. Compare to multimode fiber.

Single precision: A limit to the precision of a number based on a predetermined computer word length. See double precision.

Sixel: A column of six pixels on the screen.

SNA: system network architecture. IBM's model for inter-computer communication.

Socket: A logical entity within the node of a network.

Soft character sets: See downloadable character sets.

Sorting: The ordering of records in a particular sequence.

Source code: See compiler.

Source file: A text file with material ready for translation into an object module by an assembler or compiler.

Spooler: A piece of software that takes over a section of the computer's main memory (RAM) and uses it as storage for tasks underway such as printing or plotting. The hardware equivalent is called a buffer.

Star: A network topology in which all communication goes from the individual nodes to a central station for control.

Start bit: A serial data communications bit that informs the system that the following bits are data.

Starting address: See address.

Static memory: RAM memory using "flip-flops" as the memory elements. Data is thus retained for as long as power is applied to the flip-flops. Does not require regular refreshes. Contrast with dynamic RAM.

Status line: A line of information that appears on many terminals in many applications to advise information about the operating modes of the terminal.

Stop bit: A serial data communications bit that indicates the end of a block of data.

String: A connected series of characters.

Subdirectory: A subsidiary directory linked to a higher-level directory. For example, a system could have a directory containing a word processing program and a subdirectory beneath that directory containing memos and another subdirectory with letters.

Subprocess: A subsidiary process created by a process.

Subrate data: In a digital telephone network, data transmission at speeds less than 56 kilobits per second, including standard modem rates of 300, 1200, 2400, 4800 and 9600 baud.

Subroutine: A routine that executes when called by another routine.

Subscript: The positioning of a character or set of characters a fraction of an inch beneath the rest of the copy on a line. Often used in scientific and mathematical notation. A superscript is the positioning of a character or characters a fraction above the rest of copy on a line.

Superscript: See subscript.

Suspension: A state in which a process is inactive, but remains known to the system. It will become active if another process requests the operating system to resume it. Contrast with hibernation.

Swapping: Sharing memory resources among several processes by writing an entire working set to secondary storage (swapping out) and reading another working set into memory (swapping in). Contrast with paging.

Switch: In telecommunications, a system for controlling the routing of transmission signals entering and leaving a central office or toll office.

Symbiont: A process that transfers data to or from a mass storage device.

Symbol: A redefinition that represents a function or entity such as a command string or file name.

Synchronous communication: A method of data transmission in which the transmitter and receiver are synchronized so that both ends can define start and stop of data bytes. Compare to asynchronous communication.

Synchronous data link control (SDLC): An IBM protocol for data transfer.

Syntax: The grammatical form of a command.

Systems application architecture: An IBM specification for the "look and feel" applications across a network.

System board: See mother board.

System image: The image read into memory when a system is first started up.

System network architecture: See SNA.

System password: The password asked of the user before login can begin.

Target node: The node that is to receive a memory image from another node.

T interface: The four-wire physical link between ISDN terminal gear, limited to a distance of about a mile and a half.

Task: In network terms, an image running in the context of a process.

TCP/IP: Transmission control protocol/internet protocol. A communication protocol, developed by the Department of Defense, for connection of heterogeneous computers and networks. Used in many UNIX-based networks as well as other systems.

Telemetry: Remote measurement or recording of data using communications channels between sensing devices and the computer or data recorder.

Teletext: One-way broadcast of video images in page format, based on images and data stored in a central computer database. Contrast to videotex.

Throughput: The amount of work that can be accomplished by a particular device in a particular time period. The fact that a printer, for example, claims a speed of 100 cps does not mean that it will print 10,000 characters in 100 seconds because it will be slowed down by other factors such as the speed of the incoming data, the amount of time the printer loses because of the need to change directions or return its print head, and paper handling time losses. Also used as a measure of the effective speed of a network.

Timeout: The expiration of the time limit given a device or a user to provide a particular input.

Timesharing: A means of allocating computer time by dividing up access to the processor into equal-sized slices and then sharing it among contending processes.

Toggle: A key with an "on/off" function. Pressing the key once turns a particular feature or mode on; pressing the key a second time turns the feature or mode off. Examples include the hold screen and shift lock keys.

Token-passing: A protocol design in which an electronic token circulates around a network; nodes find an available token and attach to it. The process is used for network communication to regulate access. A station seeking to transmit waits until a token message arrives, indicating availability of the network. The data is attached to the token and sent out on the network. Other stations cannot transmit until the token is freed.

Token-ring: A design of a network in which tokens circulate around a true or logical ring structure. Described by IEEE 802.3 standards.

Toll office: A long-distance switching facility serving trunk lines to other toll offices, or to other central offices, allowing the switching of voice channels to complete a circuit from subscriber to subscriber.

Topology: The physical layout of a network in physical electrical or logical terms.

Tracks: The concentric circles of data on a formatted disk. See formatting.

Transmission control program/internet program. See TCP/IP.

Transparent: Performance of functions that are not apparent to the user. For example, the user sees the result of a command, not the process of parsing and executing the command.

Transport layer: The fourth layer of the OSI model, responsible for determining the integrity of data and the formatting of data.

Trunk: A multichannel communications link used to connect two switching offices in a network or to link a central office to a PBX.

Turnkey account: See captive account.

Twisted-pair wiring: A type of electrical cabling made from a pair of wires twisted together in a particular design to provide electrical self shielding. Many local telephone cables are twisted-pair in design.

Two's complement: A means of representing an integer in binary code in which a negative number is one greater than the bit complement of the positive number.

Type-ahead: The ability of a terminal to accept typed-in commands and data while the computer is processing a previously entered command. Input is held in a type-ahead buffer.

Universal symbol: A global symbol in a shareable image that can be used by any module linked to the image.

UNIX: An operating system with multiuser and multitasking abilities in use on large computers and on the new generation of 16-bit microcomputers. A variant of UNIX, called Xenix, is available for the PC-AT.

User authorization file: A system file created by the system manager to identify and grant access to the system for users. Included is user name, password, default account, quotas, limits, and privileges for each user.

User identification code: A 32-bit value given to users or files and other activities.

User name: The name of the user entered into the system at login.

Utility: A program with functions related to the management of a system, account, or program.

Variable: Items or events that can take on differing numeric values dependent upon other events or items.

VAX/VMS: Virtual address extension/virtual memory system.

Version number: In a file specification, it represents the various revisions of a file since creation. The lowest version number is the oldest iteration of the file. In software terms, it represents the revision level of the product. In general, software version numbers are given as a decimal number such as 4.25 in which the numbers to the left of the decimal represent major changes while differences in the number to the right of the decimal stand for bug fixes or minor alterations and improvements.

Videotex: A two-way transmission system using a telephone network to transmit and receive data and graphics to and from a central computer. Compare to teletext.

Virtual address: A 32-bit integer that identifies the location of a byte in virtual address space.

Virtual address space: All possible virtual addresses that an image executing in the context of a process can seek or store information or instructions.

Virtual circuit: A temporary data communications link between two computers that creates the effect of a dedicated link.

Virtual memory: The storage locations in physical memory and on disk that are referred to by virtual addresses. As far as the program is concerned, all storage locations appear to be locations in physical memory.

VLSI: Very-large-scale integration. The integation of more than 2,000 logic gates or more than 16 kilobits of memory on a single chip.

Voiceband data transmission: In telephone networks, a digital signal or 64 kilobits or less per second, carried on the standard 4 kilohertz bandwidth of a voice channel.

Voltage connect switch: A slide switch on many VT terminal models that allows selection of 110 volt (U.S. domestic power source) or 220 volts (many foreign countries.) In addition to the voltage connect switch setting, most terminals require the proper fuse and power cord to be installed.

Volume: A mass storage medium such as a disk pack or magnetic tape. On a PC system, a piece of storage medium formatted for files that may be a disk or a part of a disk.

VT compatibility: A claim by a third-party manufacturer to provide a functional equivalent to one of the "official" VT terminals manufactured by Digital Equipment Corp. Compatibles typically are less expensive than Digital products or provide enhanced features, or both. Compatibility does not always mean exact duplication—terminals may look different, the on-screen character display may be non-standard, and even some of the keyboard keycaps and key locations may be different. Buyers are advised to examine and test "compatibles" to be sure they meet particular needs.

VT52 Mode: A terminal setting that conforms with the official definition, by Digital Equipment Corp., of the VT52 terminal series. This mode employs Digital's proprietary text functions only.

VT100 Mode: A terminal setting that conforms with the official definition, by Digital Equipment Corp., of the VT100 terminal series. This mode employs standard ANSI functions as well as the full range of VT200 capabilities. The VT100 superseded the earlier VT52 terminal series and includes within it most of the earlier series' abilities as well.

VT200 Mode: A terminal setting that conforms with the official definition, by Digital Equipment Corp., of the VT200 terminal series. This mode employs standard ANSI functions as well as the full range of VT200 capabilities. The VT200 superseded the earlier VT100 and VT52 terminal series and includes within it most of the earlier series' abilities as well.

VTAM: Virtual telecommunications access method. Telecommunications software for MVS (Multiple Virtual Storage) machines.

Wait: A process enters a wait state and becomes inactive when it suspends itself, hibernates, or declares to the system that it needs to wait for an event or resource.

Wake: To reactivate a hibernating process.

WAN: Wide area network. A data communications network that connects computers and terminals dispersed over a wide area, often through the linkage of several LANS, or local area networks.

Wide area network: See WAN.

Wildcard: A non-alphanumeric character used in a file name or directory in a file specification to indicate "all."

Window: An object on a window display that presents information or messages.

Word: Two contiguous bytes, 16 bits in total, with bits numbered from 0 to 15, right to left. The address of the word is the address of the byte containing bit 0. When interpreted as a number, a word is a two's complement integer (bit

15 is the sign bit in a signed integer). As a signed bit, a word ranges from $-32,768$ to $32,767$. When interpreted as an unsigned integer, the value is in the range from 0 to 65,535.

Working set: The set of pages in process space that an executing process can refer to without generating a page fault. Remaining pages of the process, if any, are in memory or in secondary storage.

World: All users, including system operators, system managers, and users in an owner's group and any other group.

X.25: A protocol that specifies the interface for packet mode communication on data networks. Examples include telenet and tymnet networks.

Index